Peg Stickrod
Box 152
Farnhamville, IA 5053

S0-AGM-001

Letter Perfect

A Guide to
Practical Proofreading

Peggy Smith

EEI, located in Alexandria, VA, provides publication design, editorial, and production services, as well as training in these areas. EEI also publishes *The Editorial Eye,* a subscription newsletter focusing on standards and practices of excellence in publications, and the following books for writers and editors:

> *Mark My Words: Instruction and Practice in Proofreading,* by Peggy Smith

> *Substance & Style: Instruction and Practice in Copyediting,* by Mary Stoughton

> *Stet! Tricks of the Trade for Writers and Editors,* edited by Bruce O. Boston

© 1995 Margherita S. Smith. All rights reserved.

ISBN 0-935012-17-6

Library of Congress Cataloging-in-Publication Data

Smith, Peggy

> Letter perfect: a guide to practical proofreading/by Peggy Smith.

> > p.   cm.

> "An easy, sensible method for catching and marking errors in all types of business and professional documents."

> Includes index.

> > 1. Proofreading.   I. Title.

Z254.S6527   1995

686.2'255—dc20   95-20246

                                                                                                                CIP

For information about buying this book in quantity or to receive a catalog of other books that EEI publishes, write, telephone, or fax the publisher:

66 Canal Center Plaza, Suite 200
Alexandria, VA 22314-5507
(703) 683-0683
Fax (703) 683-4915

Acknowledgments

I'm grateful to many of the talented people at EEI, including Claire Kincaid, publisher, for her open-minded support; Andrea Sutcliffe, best of editors, for her open-hearted wisdom and cheerful counsel; Pat Caudill, quality control manager, for her eagle eye; and Jayne Sutton, project manager, for her triumph over the perils of production.

I'm also grateful to friends and family, particularly to Mary Bodnar for scrupulously reviewing the manuscript and page proofs, Howard Simmons for devising the balance sheet in Practice 24, and Timothy Smith for solving a dilemma by suggesting a "Tell 'em what you're gonna tell 'em; tell 'em; tell 'em what you told 'em" approach.

Part Three
Increasing Your Know-how

Part Four
Becoming Expert

Part Five
Summary

15. Practical Proofreading—A Summary of the Marks

Appendixes

Part One

Introduction to Practical Proofreading

1. What Practical Proofreading Is About

Chapter 1

What Practical Proofreading Is About

What Can You Learn from This Book?

This book, designed for use by anyone who must sometimes proofread, is a how-to book. It aims first to teach you how to catch the kinds of errors and problems that appear in type by presenting them one by one and providing step-by-step practice exercises to train your eye.

Next, this book aims to teach you how to mark the errors and problems you catch so the person who will correct them will know what to do. The marking system, a simplified and updated version of the professional system that has been used for centuries, is designed to be precise but flexible, easy to learn, and easy to understand.

Finally, this book aims to serve as a reference to help you expand your knowledge and your ability to find solutions to problems that are new to you. For example, if you need to look up the time-honored professional marks, Appendix B lists them.

What Is Proofreading?

Proofreading can take either of two forms:

- Comparison proofreading

- Direct proofreading.

Comparison proofreading involves comparing, word for word, a new version of a document against an older version to catch and mark the differences. For example, a proofreader might compare a handwritten draft against the pages typed from it or a typed article against the manuscript it was copied from.

Direct proofreading (without comparison) involves reading only one version of a document. This is done when only one version exists or when the older version of a document is unavailable or is difficult to use. For example, only one version exists when a business letter comes directly from a computer or when an author sends a computer disk to a publisher who will convert the text electronically to typeset pages. And only one version is readily usable when a document's original words are on audiotape.

In comparison proofreading, the main emphasis is on catching errors made in copying. Reading the new version without carefully comparing it with the old one is seldom good enough. The new version might make sense, but important changes and omissions from the old version can go undetected.

In either comparison or direct proofreading, a proofreader is seldom expected to do more than catch obvious errors in the use of language and type. Material needing much rewriting, reorganizing, or reformatting usually needs more authority than is implied by the term *proofreading*.

The most important aims of proofreading are (1) catching errors and problems and (2) marking them so whoever makes the corrections will understand what to do.

Professionally done, proofreading is a skill that requires extensive training, practice, and knowledge of typography and publication processes.[1] If you don't work as a professional proofreader, you probably do not need to know all these things. However, you may often be asked to check a document to make sure it contains no errors. The techniques in this book will help you meet these practical everyday proofreading needs.

Who Can Use Practical Proofreading Techniques?

Practical Proofreading is for people in an office of any kind whose work does not involve publishing in the formal sense.

It is for you if you must check letters, reports, financial documents, mailing lists, in-house newsletters, proposals, or technical papers.

It is for you if you must check what has been typed from your draft or your dictation.

It is for you if you are a writer or a typist or a word processing operator who proofreads your own work or that of fellow workers.

It is for you if you are a typing or word processing supervisor who checks your subordinates' work.

---

[1] If you want to know more about professional proofreading, you need my book *Mark My Words: Instruction and Practice in Proofreading*. Write or phone EEI, 66 Canal Center Plaza, Suite 200, Alexandria, VA 22314-5507, (800) 683-8380 or (703) 683-0683; fax (703) 683-4915.

It is also for you if you are a student who must proofread your own writing—or that of fellow students.

This kind of proofreading is *not* for you if you proofread printer's proofs (galleys or page proofs) for publication and are expected to use the professional system of proofmarks (see Appendix B, Professional Editing Marks and Proofmarks).

What Are the Advantages of the Practical Proofreading System?

The system taught in this book has these advantages:

- Most people who need to proofread can learn this system in just a few hours.

- Most people who will be making the corrections can learn these marks in a few minutes—they're simple, sensible, and easy to understand.

- Proofreading by this system is adaptable to any kind of typing, typesetting, or printing, including word processing and computer output.

- This system can be used to mark any kind of error.

What Makes Good Proofreading?

Good proofreading comes from knowledge, know-how, judgment, and vigilance.

Knowledge

The *knowledge* required is twofold: of language and of type—that is, of words and their symbols. It's important to pay attention both to the way words and thoughts are put together and to the way they look on a page.

You already have considerable knowledge of the English language; you use it every day. But if you are used to reading for the thought or the story, you probably see what *should be* on the page instead of errors that *are* there. The exercises in this book are designed to train your eye to catch some of the ways language can be misused in print—in typos and misspellings, for example.

You may not know a great deal about type—the way words are presented on paper. Because of the capabilities of computers, typography is no longer a province reserved for specialists. This book gives the novice some basic typographic knowledge.

Know-how

Know-how includes

1. Knowing how the documents you work on are produced and corrected

2. Knowing what errors to look for and how to find them

3. Knowing how to mark the errors and problems so they will be properly corrected

4. Knowing how to work efficiently.

It may take some research to find out how the documents you proofread are produced and corrected; you may need to ask questions and even persuade those you work with to let you observe the process closely. For example, knowing that the person making corrections has decided to completely retype a page with many changes will alert you to the need to proofread the entire page, not just the marked corrections.

Part One, Introduction to Practical Proofreading, which you are now reading, describes the structure and the aims of the Practical Proofreading system.

Part Two, Finding and Marking Problems, presents instruction and practice in the ways to correct six problems:

- Taking out type

- Adding type

- Replacing wrong characters

- Changing typeface or type style

- Adding or taking out space

- Changing the position or placement of type.

Note that half of the corrections needed are changes in language and half are changes in typography.

As the practice exercises train your eye to recognize these problems one by one, chapter by chapter, you will become a better proofreader. And as you master the marks, you will make things easier for yourself and for the person who must interpret your marks.

Part Three, Increasing Your Know-how, provides information and advice on methods and procedures, including the following:

- How to proofread solo, with a partner, with a tape recorder, and with the help of a computer

- How to write queries (questions to the writer or the person responsible for a document)

- What kinds of errors to catch in language: spelling, grammar, usage, logical thought

- How to understand typographic specifications

- How to recognize common examples of bad quality in type, such as unacceptable word division.

Part Four, Becoming Expert, goes more deeply into the aspects of proofreading for clearer language and better typography and includes tips on proofreading tables.

Judgment

Judgment is required to balance the demands of efficiency and effectiveness—neither too sloppy nor too persnickety for the job at hand. Experience is the best teacher here.

Vigilance

Vigilance is something that can't be taught. But it's easier to be vigilant if you recognize the value of the work. Remind yourself often that good proofreading can turn a badly written, badly produced document into an acceptable one and a good document into an excellent one, but bad proofreading can ruin a well-written, well-edited, well-designed document.

Choose Your Level

The knowledge and know-how in this book may be more—or less—than you are looking for. The Practical Proofreading system lets you work at the level needed. Here is how to limit or extend the skills this book teaches:

D level—If your proofreading is only casual, and if you work with experienced writers, standard formats, and knowledgeable typists or typesetters, it may be enough for you just to learn the marking system described in Chapter 15. It would also be a good idea to read through this entire book, even if you do none of the exercises.

C level—To acquire the practical skills you need for most everyday jobs, you should read and absorb the twelve chapters in Parts One, Two, and Three, doing all the exercises in those parts. It would also be a good idea to read through the rest of the book so you know where to find the specialized information should you need it.

B level—To achieve a high level of skill for nearly any kind of proofreading, you need to absorb the entire book—the fifteen chapters in Parts One through Five.

A level—Once you have mastered Practical Proofreading, you will have a foundation you can build on to achieve professional quality—for example, to work for a publisher. The resources listed in Appendix A can help you on the way to further study on the fine points of English, production, and typography.

►Tips on Proofreading

- Try to put yourself enough outside the context of what you're reading so you can catch anomalies, but not enough to miss the sense of a sentence. According to *The Mind,* a volume in the Life Science Library, "Many psychological experiments have given abundant proof of the fact that often we see what we expect to see.... If the word 'chack' is inserted in a sentence about poultry-raising, a proofreader is apt to misread it as 'chick.' If it appears in a sentence about banking, it will be misread as 'check.'" Catching *chacks* is the sign of an alert worker.

- Observe and analyze the idiosyncrasies of the individual authors, typists, and typesetters whose work you proofread. Each one's work can usually be identified—and better proofread—by knowing its characteristic errors. For example, one typesetter may often set *es* instead of *ed* at the end of a word. Another may set twenty error-free paragraphs and then suddenly make four typos in one sentence.

2. Getting Ready

Chapter 2

Getting Ready

Needed Supplies

You need the following items to do the exercises in this book:

- A good light
- A flat or slanted surface with enough space for you to work comfortably
- A pen or pencil that marks in a conspicuous color contrasting with the black type
- A recent standard dictionary
- A book that explains basic rules of grammar and punctuation.

Terms to Know Before You Start

Key Words

Copy (as a noun): (1) *The copy* is the written material, as in "handwritten copy," "typed copy," and "typeset copy." (2) *A copy* is a reproduction or duplicate of an original work.

Lowercase letters are the small letters of the alphabet; *capitals* or *caps* (or *uppercase*) are the block letters.

this is a line of lowercase letters
THIS IS A LINE OF CAPITAL LETTERS

A *character* is any single letter of the alphabet, a punctuation mark, a numeral, or a symbol (such as a dollar sign).

> ***Avoid proofreading on a computer screen.*** On a printout, you'll catch many more errors—perhaps because type on paper (hard copy) seems stable and respectable compared with the impermanent image on a computer screen (soft copy).

> **Walk before you run.** Learn first to proofread with great accuracy. When you find and mark everything you should, push toward speed.

A *subscript* is a character that goes below the line. For example, the $_2$ in H_2O is a subscript.

A *superscript* is a character that goes above the line. Footnote references are often superscripts. The ^{2} in $3^2 = 9$ is a superscript.

Type (noun) is a collection of characters put on paper (or other material) mechanically or electronically. Typewriters, word processors, computers, and specialized typesetting equipment all produce type.

To type (verb) is to work on a keyboard that produces type—for example, on the keyboard of a typewriter, word processor, or computer.

Typeset copy has many more variables than copy from a traditional typewriter. For example, a page may be set with several type sizes and typefaces (see the next section). Many refinements are available, such as true quotation marks (as in "quote") instead of inch symbols (as in "quote") and true dashes (—) as well as hyphens (-) or double hyphens (--).

Typeset characters are spaced proportionally—that is, a *W* takes more horizontal space than an *i,* and an *O* takes more space than a period. Traditional typewriter characters are monospaced—that is, each one takes the same amount of space.

Typeset style: ABCDEFGHIJKLMNOPQRSTUVWXYZ
abcdefghijklmnopqrstuvwxyz

Typewriter style: ABCDEFGHIJKLMNOPQRSTUVWXYZ
abcdefghijklmnopqrstuvwxyz

Typefaces

You need to know a few terms for typefaces:

Roman type is standard, upright type. You see it in books and newspapers.

This is a line of roman type.

Italic type is slanted. It is used for emphasis and for titles and headings.

This is a line of italic type.

Boldface type is heavier type with thicker lines. Boldface can be either italic or roman.

This is a line of boldface roman type.
This is a line of boldface italic type.

Abbreviations

You need to know these abbreviations:

p.:　　page (for example, "Move text to p. 21.")

pp.:　　pages (for example, "Refer to pp. 2–9.")

cap(s):　capital letter(s)

lc:　　lowercase

sc:　　small capitals (small caps), which are usually 70 percent of the size of full caps, are not available in typewriter-style type but may be called for in typeset copy.

THIS IS A LINE IN FULL CAPS

THIS IS A LINE IN SMALL CAPS

Some of these abbreviations may be combined:

caps + lc:　capitals and lowercase

This Is a Line in Caps and Lowercase

caps + sc:　caps and small caps

THIS IS A LINE IN CAPS AND SMALL CAPS

sp:　　an instruction to spell out a short form—that is, an abbreviation, numeral, or symbol. (It doesn't mean "correct the spelling.") Here are examples of short and spelled-out forms:

Short Form	*Spelled-out Form*
U.S.	United States
22	twenty-two
10%	ten percent
©	copyright

Five General Rules for Practical Proofreading

Rule 1. Mark Only on Material You Will Not Harm

For Practical Proofreading, you need to make proofmarks directly on the page. Do not, however, mark an original that cannot be replaced. Mark only on printouts or hard copy (from a computer or word processor), photocopies, or other kinds of copies.

If you have only the original of something, such as a form filled out on a typewriter, address labels, or camera-ready copy (pages ready to be photographed and printed), make a photocopy to mark on.

Rule 2. Write Clearly and Mark Neatly

Practical Proofreading fails if your marks are hard to see or your handwriting can be misread.

If your cursive or "script" handwriting is good, use it. But if anyone has ever complained that your handwriting is hard to read, you must print. For printing, form your letters and numbers like these:

Block capitals: A B C D E F G H I J K L M
N O P Q R S T U V W X Y Z

Lowercase: a b c d e f g h i j k l m
n o p q r s t u v w x y z

Numbers: 1 2 3 4 5 6 7 8 9 0

Note: When *l* and *r* stand alone, use the written forms ℓ and r; they are easier to read accurately.

Whether you write or print, space your characters so that no one can mistake one word for two or two words for one, and be sure to make capitals distinctly larger than lowercase letters.

Write exactly what you want to see; for example, don't write an ampersand (⅊ or &) if you want the spelled-out word *and,* and don't write in capital letters except where you want them.

Don't mark so heavily that you can't read what's underneath.

Rule 3. Use a Marking System Suited to the Space Available Between Lines

Text Marks. Use text marks when the space between lines is large enough to write in without crowding. Mark right in the line of type to show *where* a change is needed; then, to show *what* change is needed, mark in the empty space above the type with the error.

The characters you write should be about the same size as or larger than the type characters on the page. If you judge the blank space between lines to be about the same height as a line of type (from the top of a capital letter to the bottom of a lowercase *g*, *p*, or *y*), the space is adequate for marks between the lines.

Text marks look like this:

> Beat it on the drum-o,
>
> Play it on the pipe-o:
>
> Every single writ*t*en word's
>
> P*o*tentially a typo.

Margin Marks. Use margin marks when space between lines is too tight for text marks. Mark in the line of type to show *where* a change is needed; then, to show *what* change is needed, mark in the margin closer to the error:

> Beat it on the drum-o,
> Play it on the pipe-o:
> Every single writen word's   *t*
> *o* Patentially a typo.

The proofmarks used by professional proofreaders are margin marks. Nearly all the practice exercises in this book, however, require text marks because they are more common—and more useful—in Practical Proofreading.

Rule 4. Write Instructions in the Margin and Draw a Ring Around Them

A ring around a mark in the margin is called a *message ring;* it means "Follow these instructions but don't type or typeset the characters here." Use the message ring for either text marks or margin marks.

First, mark in the text; then, in the margin, write the explanation of what you want done and draw a ring around the explanation.

The message ring is very useful. Use it when the character you want could be misunderstood or when you need to tell the person making the corrections exactly what to do:

(*zero*)   20,000 Leagues Under the Sea

(*ital, not BF*)   Not every (aloha) is a hello.

Use it when characters could be confused with others or when they are not on a standard keyboard.

$$2^2 = 4, \quad 4^2 = 16, \quad 16^2 = 256 \qquad \text{(superscript)}$$

> ***An extreme reaction to bad proofreading:***
>
> "In his *Memoirs,* Baron de Grimm tells of a French author who died in a spasm of anger after he had detected more than three hundred typographical errors in a newly printed copy of his work."
>
> **—De Vinne**

Here are examples using the message ring:

Text with Error	Mark in Text	Mark in Margin	Corrected Copy
S75	$75	*(dollar sign)*	$75
No. 3	No. 3	*(number sign)*	# 3
one %	one %	*(figure 1)*	1 %

Rule 5. Read for Meaning as Well as for Errors

Good proofreading is a complex process: You look for problems large and small in the use of language as well as problems in the use of type. It's something like observing the forest, the trees, and every little leaf all at once. Few people can see both the whole picture and the details in just one read-through.

You'll do well to proofread everything at least three times:

- First, proofread to catch errors in spelling, grammar, and usage.

- Second, proofread to catch departures from good typographic practice, such as bad breaks at the ends of lines or pages, mis-alignment, or inconsistent spacing between characters, words, or lines.

- Third, proofread to be sure everything makes sense—the words in their context and in their presentation in type.

▶Tips on Preparing to Proofread

- There's a way out if you can't simply erase or cross out a mark made in error (for example, when you've used a pen to mark incorrectly for something to be taken out). Use the very helpful message "stet," a Latin word meaning "Let it stand" or "Ignore the mark; leave the copy the way it was before it was marked."

  Here's how to stet a mistake: Put dots under the text mark, cross out the margin mark (if there is one), and write "stet" in a message ring in the margin, like this:

   ~~proof~~readers reading proof

- Before you proofread a document with more than one page, do one important minor chore: Make sure all the pages are numbered and in sequence. If the pages aren't numbered, number them—on their backs if you don't want the numbers to show. If you are proofreading by comparison, check the page numbers of both the old and the new versions. You need to be sure all the pages are there, and you also need to be able to put the pages back in order if they get mixed up.

- If you're not the author, be sure you have a good reason for every change you introduce. The greatest sins are introducing error, changing the meaning, and making needless changes.

Part Two

Finding and Marking Problems

3. Taking Out Type

Chapter 3

Taking Out Type

How to Mark to Take Out Type

Marking to take out type is simple. The best way to do it depends on how long the take-out is.

One Character

To take out one character, slash through it and draw a loop at the top of the slash ( ). Do not black out the character, because the person making the correction must be able to read it. For example, to take out an unwanted *y,* mark as shown:

proofready

More than One Character

To take out more than one character, a whole word, or an entire line, mark a horizontal line through everything that must go. Be careful to mark out neither more nor less than you mean to. Be sure that what you mark out can still be read.

 ~~proof~~proofreading

It's a good idea to add a loop to the strikethrough. The loop is useful in several ways:

- The symbol is well known: Lists of professional editor's marks and proofmarks all show a form of the loop as a take-out sign.

- The take-out loop calls attention to the mark, which might otherwise be overlooked.

> ***If it's as plain as the nose on your face, everybody can see it but you.***
> Where is the reader most likely to notice errors? On a title page; in a header; in a caption; in the first line, first paragraph, or first page of copy; and in the top lines of a new page. These are precisely the places where editors and proofreaders are most likely to miss errors. Take extra care at every beginning.

Mistakery loves company. Errors frequently cluster. When you find one, look hard for others nearby.

■ When it's marked in the middle of a word, turning upward and looping above the line, the loop can show exactly where a take-out stops (or starts):

What's sauce for the goose is applesauce for the gander.
Don't change horseshoes in midstream.

Several Lines

To take out several entire, consecutive lines, just strike through each line and end with a take-out loop:

Now is the time
for all good men
and all good women
and all good men
and all good women
to come to the aid
of their country.

A Long Passage

To take out a long passage or a whole page, draw a box around it, mark a big X through it, and write a large take-out loop in the margin:

To take out a long passage or a whole page, draw a box around it, mark a big X through it, and write a large take-out loop in the margin:

Marks for Taking Out Type

Mark	Meaning	Example	Corrected Copy
Short Take-out			
Looped strike-through	Take out a word or several characters	abc def ghi xxx jkl mxxxno pqr	abc def ghi jkl mno pqr
Looped slash	Take out one character	abc dxef ghi	abc def ghi
Long Take-out			
Big X plus take-out loop	Take out an entire passage	abc def ghi jkl mno pqr stu stu abc def ghi jkl mno pqr vwx yz	abc def ghi jkl mno pqr stu vwx yz

▶ Tips for Taking Out Type

- Ordinarily, you should not try to mark for the new spacing that may be needed once characters are taken out. Leave these spacing changes to the typist or typesetter.

- Repetitions are frequent sources of error. Look out for—

  - repeated characters—watch especially for the tall ones in the middle of a word (litt~~l~~le, midd~~d~~le)

  - repeated words—watch especially at the start of a line (start of ~~of~~ a line)

  - repeated passages, which can occur when a typist's eyes jump back to similar characters on a computer screen or on a document being copied—and which you can miss when your eyes make the same jump. In the following example, the typist's eyes jumped back to the word *Mary:*

    Mary had a little lamb, its fleece was white as snow, and every-where that Mary had a little lamb, its fleece was white as snow, and everywhere that Mary went, the lamb was sure to go.

- Take care that strikethroughs stop (or start) short of punctuation that needs to stay in place.

  Don't buy a pig in a poke~~r game~~.

Repeated Characters

If you need to take out characters, words, or lines that are repeated by mistake, you have to decide which set to mark.

You should mark excess characters at the beginnings and ends of words to leave the words whole:

> A good ~~begin~~beginning makes a good ending.
> A good beginning makes a good ending~~ding~~.

It seldom matters which repetition you mark out in the middle of a word or sentence (or which entire line you mark out). In these examples, either choice would be correct:

> Thi~~n~~nk!
> Thin~~n~~k!

> ~~Practice~~ Practice makes perfect.
> Practice ~~Practice~~ makes perfect.

How to Work the Exercises

Practice exercises in this book will help you remember what you have read.

A good way to learn proofreading (or nearly anything) is by doing it while you tell yourself what you are doing. Talk to yourself as you work the exercises. For example, while you work the first line of Practice 1, say, "To take out the extra 3, I slash through it and add a take-out loop." As you continue, you might shorten the conversation to "Slash, take-out loop. Slash, take-out loop."

This is a good technique for self-study. Try it!

When you have finished an exercise, compare your marks one by one with the answer key in Appendix C. Analyze the kinds of errors you missed, notice which marks you made wrong, and invent your own corrective exercises.

Practice 1. Taking Out Type (Direct Proofreading)

Instructions: Mark the following for correction. Use text marks.
Compare your work with the answer key in Appendix C.

A. Alphabet and Numbers

1 2 3 3 4 5 6 7 8 9 10 11 12 13 144 15 16 17 18 19 20

a b x c d e f g h i j k y l m n o p q r s t z u v w x y z

1970

19710

1972

1973

1837

1974

1975

1976

121977

B. Old Chinese Proverb

What your see, you forget.

What you heard, you rememember.

What you do, you do understand.

C. Brokern Patterns

Proofreading is little more than searching for broken pattterns. Of
course, to be able to detect a broken pattern, Of course, to be able
to detect a broken pattern, a good proofreader has to fully under-
understand what the pattern is. That takes two kinds of aware-
nesss—of language and off type.

Comparison Proofreading

When you proofread by comparison, you look for the same things as in direct proofreading, but you also look for mistakes in copying.

The exercises in comparison proofreading in this book are meant for you to work on by yourself.[1] To help ensure accuracy, keep your place by using a ruler to follow the old version line by line while your pencil follows the new copy word by word. Start by reading only seven or eight words at a time. It helps to read aloud—in a whisper if need be.

---

[1] Chapter 11 discusses comparison proofreading with a partner or with a tape recorder.

Practice 2. Taking Out Type (Comparison Proofreading)

Instructions: Mark the column on the right to match the column on the left. Use text marks. Compare your work with the answer key in Appendix C.

Comparison Proofreading Yesterday and Today

Before computers entered the process, a manuscript destined for publication was copied by typing on a keyboard, letter by letter, using a typewriter or typesetting equipment.

Proofreaders would then compare the newly typed or typeset version, letter by letter, with the manuscript.

In most cases today, computers have eliminated the age-old tradition of comparison proofreading. Word processed material is corrected error by error—without being entirely retyped. Typewritten or typeset material can be transferred electronically to a computer through a text scanner and then corrected error by error—without being entirely retyped. The electronic files can later be converted for use in desktop publishing or typesetting programs.

But errors can creep in during electronic conversion, often in the form of misread characters or dropped words or lines. And still today documents or parts of documents may be entirely retyped. It's still important to verify accuracy by comparing a final copy with an earlier version.

Before computers entered the process, a manuscript destined for publications was copied by typeing on a a keyboard, letter by letter, using a typewriter or typesetting equipment.

Proofreaders would then compare the newly typed or typeset version, letter by letter, with the manuscript.

In most all cases today, computers have eliminated the age-old tradition of comparison proofreading. Word-processed material is corrected error by error—without its being entirely retyped. Typewritten or or typeset materials can be transferred electronically to a computer thorough a text scanner, and then corrected error by error—without out being entirely retyped. The electronic files can later be converted for use in desktop publishing or typesetting programs.

But errors can creep in during electronic conversion, often in the forum of misread characters or dropped words or lines. And still today documents or parts of documents may be entirely retyped. It's still today documents or parts of documents may be entirely retyped. It's still .important to verify accuracy by comparing a finalized copy with an earlier version..

4. Adding Type

Chapter 4

Adding Type

How to Mark to Add Type

Marking to add type is simple. First make a pointer (a caret)—like this ∧ —in the text, pointing up to the place in the line where the addition belongs. The next step depends on how long the addition is.

Short Additions

To add just a few characters or words (up to six words or a single short line), first mark a pointer in the text where the addition belongs. Next write the addition above the line:

mis∧pelling

You need only one pointer no matter how many characters or words are needed:

can't
Nothing you ∧ spell will ever work.—Will Rogers

Long Additions

Long additions—more than one line—take special treatment.

In direct proofreading, here's how to handle a long addition:

1. First, mark a pointer where the long addition belongs. Next, write this message in the space between lines above the pointer:

    (add attached)

2. Provide the attachment by writing or typing it on a separate page labeled like this:

    (add to p. x)

> **The footbone conneckit to the knee bone?** Numerical and alphabetical sequences often go awry. Check for omissions and duplications in page numbers, footnote numbers, or notations in outlines and lists. Check any numeration, anything in alphabetical order, and everything sequential (such as the path of arrows in a flowchart).

35

If you find very few errors, it's time to worry that some were missed; if you find a great many errors, it's time to worry that even more were missed.

If there's more than one long addition on a page, use an "ABC" key, for example:

1. Write this message: (add A, attached)

2. Label the first addition Ⓐ, the second Ⓑ, and so on.

In comparison proofreading, here are examples of two ways to handle a long addition:

1. Mark the omission in the old version.

   ■ On the new version: First, mark a pointer in the text showing exactly where the needed addition belongs. Next, write a message in the margin—for example: (add 2 lines fr. p. 5)

   ■ On the old version: First, place a self-stick note at the top of the page containing the missing passage. Next, mark the passage plainly, using brackets or another self-stick note.

   OR

2. Make a photocopy of the omission.

   ■ Make a photocopy of the page of the old version containing the missing passage. Mark the passage plainly.

   ■ Attach the photocopy to the page of the new version where the addition is needed.

   ■ In the new version: First, mark a pointer showing exactly where the addition belongs. Next, write this message in the margin:

   (add attached)

Long Pointers

If you think it is necessary, lengthen one line of the pointer to show exactly where an addition goes:

proof‸reading

You may also add an extended bracket above the line to be sure everything in an addition is included or to separate one addition from another:

wks (last laughs)
He laughs best.

▶Tips for Adding Type

- Ordinarily, you should not mark for any obvious new spacing that may be needed. Leave these spacing changes to the typist or typesetter.

- Studies show that omissions—both of letters and of words—are by far the most common errors.

Watch especially for missing negatives—words like *no, not, don't,* and *never,* endings like *n't* in *don't* and *didn't,* and prefixes like *dis* and *un.*

Children should be seen and ^not^ heard.

No one who minds his own business is ^un^ employed.

When you do comparison proofreading, be aware that copy can be skipped when a typist's eyes jump forward to similar characters—and that your eyes can make the same jump. For example, a typist whose eyes jump from the first *lamb* to the next in the following nursery rhyme will skip a dozen words:

Mary had a little lamb, its fleece was white as snow, and everywhere that Mary went, the lamb was sure to go.

The result:

Mary had a little lamb was sure to go.

Sometimes you may need a sideways pointer to mark between lines:

```
           100
  300 >    200
           400
           500
```

If you want to show exactly where an addition goes in a column, you can lengthen one line of the sideways pointer or draw an arrow, like this:

```
        100                        100
        200                        200
  300>_____                 300 ——→
        400                        400
        500                        500
```

Close-up Hooks

If you want to be sure characters are not added to the end or beginning of the wrong word, use close-up hooks.

Close-up hooks on the right side of an addition mean "attach this on its right." For example, if you want "plan this," mark as shown:

He will plan his garden in the spring.

Close-up hooks on the left side mean "attach this on its left." For example, if you want "plant his," mark as follows:

He will plan his garden in the spring.

Use close-up hooks to be sure characters are attached to the correct group:

20   21   22   3   24   25   2   27   28   29

I   II   III   IV   V   V   VII   VIII   X   X

You don't need close-up hooks to add characters in the middle of words or to add whole words.

Marks for Adding Type

Mark	Meaning	Example	Corrected Copy
Pointer	Add the character(s) written above the line	inset	insert
Hooks	Connect the addition at its left or right as hooks show	nsert	insert
		inser	insert

Practice 3. Adding Type

A. Direct Proofreading

Instructions: Mark the following for correction. Use text marks. Compare your work with the answer key in Appendix C.

Alphabet and Numbers

a c d e f g h i j l m n o p q r s u v w x y z

1990

1991

1993

1994

1995

196

1997

998

Sentences

1. If it's not chocolate, it's not desert.

2. The queen wore a tiara of diamonds and pears.

3. The speaker asked for the audience's divided attention.

4. We advise people with high cholesterol to eat more than two eggs a week.

5. Are we suppose to get use to thinking it's too much trouble to make mash potatoes the old-fashion way?

B. Comparison Proofreading

Instructions: Mark the column on the right to match the column on the left. Ignore the difference in space between lines. (A new version often differs from an old in format.) Use text marks. Compare your work with the answer key in Appendix C.

Printers' Measure

    In traditional printers' measure, 6 picas = .99648 inch. In many desktop publishing systems, however, 6 picas = exactly 1 inch. The difference, .00352, or about 35 thousandths of an inch, is so small that you're almost always quite safe in considering 72 points equal to 1 inch.

Printers' Mesure

    In tradition printers' measure, 6 picas = .99648 inch. In many desktop publishing system, however, 6 picas = exacly 1 inch. The difference, .00352, or about 35 thousands of an inch, is so that you're most always quit safe in considering 72 pints equal to 1 inch.

Practice 4. Taking Out and Adding Type

Instructions: Mark the following for correction. Use text marks. Compare your work with the answer key in Appendix C.

Why You Should Prefer to Work on Paper

Paper is probabally what you're used to. Most people can read words on paper much more accurately than on a computer screen—and therefor can do better at catching defects in printed words.

Paper is easy to handle. You can readily take it or send it nearly anywheres; you can quick find your way through a stack of it; you can make inexpensive copies inexpensively so that each person in a group can look at and discuss they same document at the same time.

Paper allows simulation. You can mark on it to give the idea of proposed changes without actually making them.

Paper allows simulation. You can mark on it to give the idea of proposed changes without actually making them.

Paper permits commentry. You can readily distinguish between the text and the written responses to the text.

Paper provides a trail. You can see at a glance what the text was like be before it was marked up. You can review your own work and approve or disprove it. And, keeeping in mind that a writer wants—and deserves—to see hat changes have been made, you can provide a record provide a record if you've worked on someone else's writing, or you can refer to the record if someone else has worked one you writing.

5. Replacing Characters

Chapter 5

Replacing Characters

How to Mark for Replacement

To replace incorrect characters with correct ones, first mark out the incorrect characters in the text. Then write the correct characters in the line above the type.

To mark out one character for replacement, use a slash:

All the world loves a lo$\cancel{s}$er.

To mark out two or more characters, it's usually a good idea to use a strikethrough and replace the whole word:

Do this: Rome was not ~~burnt~~ *built* in a day.

Not this: Rome was not bu*il*~~rn~~t in a day.

And not this: Rome was not bu*il*rnt in a day.

✏️ ## Marks for Replacement

Mark	Meaning	Example	Corrected Copy
Slash plus replacement	Replace one character as shown above the line	repl*a*~~e~~ce	replace
Strikethrough plus replacement	Replace several characters as shown above the line	*right* ~~wrong~~ word	right word

Don't fall off the horse in the paddock or the home stretch. Errors often slip by at the beginning or end of a table, chapter, section, page, paragraph, or line, and at the beginning or end of a stint of work, even when the interruption is brief.

Note that slashes and strikethroughs used for replacement have no loop, unlike those used to mark take-outs.

One slash or strikethrough takes care of as many or as few characters or words as are needed in that spot, that is—one marked-out character or word can be replaced with several, and several words can be replaced with one.

Thirty days has September,

April, June, ~~as well as~~ November;

~~Others~~ have thirty-one...

Tips on Replacing Wrong Characters and Words

■ If you can't quickly figure out what's wrong with a word, mark through the entire word and write it correctly above the line:

proofreading
~~phooferaeding~~

■ To mark clearly, replace a whole word when two or more characters are wrong—for example, to change "forbid" to "permit,"

Good: *permit* ~~forbid~~

Too complicated: f̸or̸b̸id̸ *pe m t*

Replace only the wrong characters, however, when replacing a whole word is impractical—for example, when a long word contains wrong characters that are far apart:

Avoid ø̸vercomplicates̸ marks. *o* *d*

Do what's clear and sensible. Practical Proofreading should be, above all, practical.

■ Word processing spell checkers are useful; they catch errors and they can teach correct spelling to attentive operators. But they don't catch typos that are words. With or without spell checking, watch for words that make no sense in context.

- Did Stanley rea~~d~~y say, "Dr. Livingstone, I presume?" *ll*

- It's n̸ow or never. *n*

■ Watch for commonly confused or misused words:

- I look forward to writing the ~~forward~~ to your book. *foreword*

- Applications for staff positions ~~excepted.~~ *accepted*

Practice 5. Replacing Wrong Words and Characters with Right Ones

Instructions: Mark all the following for correction. Use text marks. Remember to replace a whole word where two or more characters in it are wrong. Compare your work with the answer key in Appendix C.

A. Alphabet and Numbers

a b x d e f g h i j k y m n o p q r s z u v w x y z

won two three fore fife six
seven ate nine tan eleven swerve

1995

1996

1997

1798

9999

2000

B. Misspelled Words

1. cause and affect

2. complementary tickets

3. the capital dome

4. a half-carrot diamond

5. grisly bear

6. holier then thou

C. Spoonerisms

"Spoonerisms" are named after their reputed source, Dr. Spooner, professor and preacher. Mark them for correction. *Example:*

This pie is occupewed. Let me sew you to another sheet.

1. Young man, you have hissed all your mystery lessons and completely tasted two whole worms.

2. It is kisstomary to cuss the bride.

3. The poor man just received a blushing crow.

4. He went to Portsmouth to see the cattleships and bruisers.

5. Have you ever nursed in your bosom a half-warmed fish?

Special Kinds of Replacement

Marking to Spell Out a Word

To replace a short form—an abbreviation, numeral, or symbol—with the spelled-out word it represents, first mark a ring around it; next, write (sp) in the margin or in the space above. "Sp" as an abbreviation for "spell out" is standard shorthand in the publications field.

> To get this:
>
> > All English words are made
> > from twenty-six letters.
>
> Do this:
>
> > All English words are made
> >
> > (sp)   from (26) letters.
>
> Or this:
>
> > All English words are made
> > from (sp 26) letters.

Note: As the example above shows, a very brief abbreviation or instruction in a message ring is acceptable in the space between lines when there is room.

When several short forms near each other need to be spelled out, you can write "sp" just once and indicate the number of times the spell-out instruction applies:

> (sp 2x)   (1) million bytes equal (1) megabyte

Sweat the small stuff. Watch strings of little words (*if it is as bad as he says...*) and watch the inside letters of words. A simple transposition turns *marital strife* into *martial strife,* *board room* into *broad room.* One missing character turns *he'll* into *hell,* *public* into *pubic.*

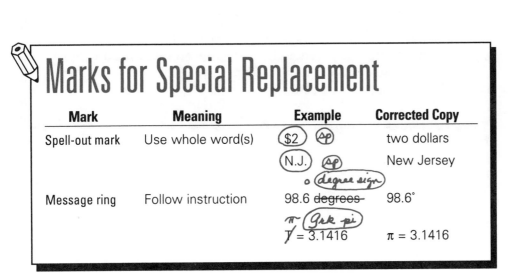

Marks for Special Replacement

Mark	Meaning	Example	Corrected Copy
Spell-out mark	Use whole word(s)	($2) (sp)	two dollars
		(N.J.) (sp)	New Jersey
Message ring	Follow instruction	98.6 ~~degrees~~ ° (degree sign)	98.6°
		π (Grk pi) / = 3.1416	π = 3.1416

Marking for a Short Form

To replace a spelled-out word with its short form, mark for simple replacement with a slash or a strikethrough, and write the correct form above the line:

16 oz. = 1 lb.
~~Sixteen ounces equal one pound~~

B.A.
~~Bachelor of Arts~~

▶ Tips on Marking for Spelling Out

- Use simple replacement when spelling out involves changes in punctuation and capitalization. Here, for example, the capital D must be lowercased and the period after "Dr." removed:

  doctor
  An apple a day keeps the ~~Dr.~~ away.

- Use simple replacement when an incorrect spelled-out form could be chosen:

Spell-out Marks	Miscorrected Copy
His Ⓒ.Ⓞ retired to Vancouver, Ⓑ.Ⓒ. Ⓢp 2x	His company retired to Vancouver, Before Christ
Precise Marks	**Intended Correction**
commanding officer His ~~C.O.~~ retired to British Columbia Vancouver, ~~B.C.~~	His commanding officer retired to Vancouver, British Columbia

- When you write an entire word above the line, be sure to make capitals large enough to distinguish them from lowercase. Chapter 8, Marking for Type Style Changes, explains how to mark single letters unmistakably.

Practice 6. Marks for Special Replacement

Follow the instructions for each section. Use text marks. Compare your work with the answer key in Appendix C.

A. Message Ring

Mark for replacement using the message ring.

1. Water freezes at 32O Fahrenheit.

2. The chemical formula for water is H to O.

3. The chemical formula for water is H2O.

4. Most keyboards show a dollar sign ($) but not a cents sign (c).

5. An English alphabet can be used to set the Spanish forms of address by adding a tilde (~) above the letter n (ñ): señor, senora, señorita.

6. "Fences" include opening and closing forms of these symbols:
   - parentheses: (and)
   - brackets: [and]
   - braces or curly brackets: { and }.

B. Long and Short Forms

Use the spell-out mark or simple replacement as needed to follow these commonly used style rules:

Spell out abbreviations and ampersands (&— also called "and-signs").
Spell out fractions, any number that begins a sentence, and whole numbers from one through nine, except for dates and prices.
Use figures (numerals) for whole numbers from 10 up.

> 500 years ago, books printed with movable type sold for about one-fifth the price of ms. books. The daybook of a Venetian bookseller in fourteen eighty-four shows a stock of classics, religious works, schoolbooks, romances, & poetry. Dante's *Inferno* cost 1 ducat; Plutarch's *Lives,* two ducats. Most customers paid cash, but Cicero's *Orations* was exchanged for wine, & other bks for oil or flour. The bookseller paid a binder with a copy of *The Life & Miracles of the Madonna,* an illuminator with an arith textbook, & a proofreader with 3 books incl a Bible.

6. Transposition

Chapter 6

Transposition

How to Mark for Transposing Type

Some people use a double curve to mark transposed (exchanged) characters or words. If this is easy for you, do it. Mark a double curve (∩∪) around the words or characters that should be exchanged.

Page to poster, to sign chart
Proofreading's both craft and rat.

Transposition, however, is a form of replacement. It's just as easy to mark such a problem as a replacement:

Do either this: The pen is mightier than the words.

Or this: The pen is mightier than the ~~words~~. *sword*

It's a poor idea to transpose numbers; they're too easily mixed up. It's better to mark to replace transposed numbers:

Poor: 19₆₇   Good: 19₆₇ *76*   Even better: ~~1967~~ *1976*

Marks for Transposition

Mark	Meaning	Example
Double curve	Transpose adjacent characters or words or move to another position	When one odor shuts, another opens.
		Birds in their nests agree little.
		abc def ghi stu vwx yz jkl mno pqr
Brackets plus arrow	Move to another position	abc def ghi stu vwx yz jkl mno pqr

You can transpose adjacent lines or paragraphs with a horizontal double curve:

> One for the money,
> Two for the show,
> And four to go.
> Three to get ready,

Another way to switch lines is to bracket the ones to be moved and mark an arrow to show where they belong:

> One for the money,
> Two for the show,
> And four to go.
> Three to get ready,

▶ Tips on Transposing

- Pay attention to punctuation marks. Mark double curves carefully to avoid moving punctuation that needs to stay where it is.

  The pen is mightier than the words.

- Keep transpositions easy to interpret. Transpositions within transpositions are confusing.

  Good: Circumstances cases later.

  Confusing: Circumstances cases later.

- Two connected double curves are confusing. If transposed words are not right next to each other, mark each for replacement.

  Good: Be dumb to kind animals.

  Confusing: Be dumb to kind animals.

- Mark to replace the whole word if transposed characters are not right next to each other:

  Good: Knowledge is porew.

  Confusing: Knowledge is porew.

  Also confusing: Knowledge is porew.

Practice 7. Transposing

Instructions: Do this exercise to practice using the special mark for transposing—the double curve. Compare your work with the answer key in Appendix C.

1. Mark "setup" to make "upset"   setup

2. Mark "hangover" to make "overhang"   hangover

3. Mark "human being" to make "being human"   human being

4. Mark "sky blue" to make "blue sky"   sky blue

5. Mark "trail" to make "trial"   trail

6. Mark "ingrain" to make "raining"   ingrain

7. Mark "casual" to make "causal"   casual

8. Mark "procede" to make "proceed"   procede

9. Mark "calvary" to make "cavalry"   calvary

10. Mark "marital" to make "martial"   marital

11. Mark "aide" to make "idea"   aide

12. Mark "stake" to make "takes"   stake

13. Mark "swing" to make "wings"   swing

14. Mark "range" to make "anger"   range

15. Mark "grate" to make "great"   grate

16. Mark "wired" to make "weird"   wired

17. Mark "parse" to make "spare"   parse

18. Mark "spare" to make "pares"   spare

19. Mark "pares" to make "pears"   pares

20. Mark "pears" to make "spear"   pears

21. Mark "spear" to make "spare"   spear

22. Mark "spare" to make "parse"   spare

Practice 8. Blatant Errors in Grammar and Usage

Glass houses invite stones. Beware copy that discusses errors. When the subject is typographical quality, the copy must be typographically perfect. When the topic is errors in grammar or spelling, the copy must be error-free. Keep alert for mistakes in words like *typographical* or *proofreading*.

Instructions: Nonstandard grammar that may be acceptable in speech is not acceptable in writing. This exercise presents some blatant problems in grammar and usage. In fact, every numbered item contains more than one error. Mark the errors with text marks. Compare your work with the answer key in Appendix C. If you don't do well on this exercise, see Appendix A for a list of resources that will help you improve your knowledge of grammar and usage.

1. You should of known that your name and address goes here.

2. I disremember whether your name or address go here.

3. Your name, as well as your address and phone number, goes here now, irregardless of where the information used to went.

4. Nothing would please her and I more than to find at last a cheese-cake for we dieters.

5. Just between you and I, I don't read all the newspaper; I only read what I like.

6. I can't hardly believe that the fire burned for nine hours and required 500 firefighters to be extinguished.

7. I heard the airplane mowing the lawn, and I watched the accident, but I couldn't do nothing to help.

8. Dear Mr. Soenso:

   This is a reminder about invoice number 9991 for $650.98 and invoice number 9991A for $1.29, which is now more than 60 days passed due. If their are any problems with these invoices, please call me at once so we can correct it.

   If your payment is in the mail, please except our thanks and disregard this letter. Thank for your busness and for you prompt attention to this matter.

   Sincerely,

   Parker Plaice

   Account Represenive

Practice 9. Review of Marks (Comparison Proofreading)

Instructions: Mark the column on the right to match the column on the left. Use text marks. Compare your marks with the answer key in Appendix C.

Proverbs	**Proverb**
1. Rats leave a sinking ship.	1. Rats leave a stinking ship.
2. Love me, love my dog.	2. Love mew, love my dog.
3. Don't count your chickens before they're hatched.	3. Don't count on chickens
4. Don't put the cart before the horse.	4. before they're hatcheted. Don't put the cat before the hose.
5. Don't throw a monkey wrench into the works.	5. Don't throw a monkey to the works.
6. Consider the ant, thou sluggard, and be wise.	6. Consider the sluggard, thou ant, and be wiser.
7. Misery loves company.	7. Misery loves sympathy.
8. Where there's a will there's a way.	8. Were there's a wall, theirs a away.
9. Fools rush in where angels fear to tread.	9. Fools rush in where angles fare to trade.
10. A cursed fiend wrought death, disease, and pain. A blessed friend brought breath and ease again.	10. A cursed fiend wrought death, disease, and pain. A cursed fiend wrought death, disease, and pain.

7. Marks for Punctuation and Symbols

Chapter 7

Marks for Punctuation and Symbols

How to Mark for Punctuation and Symbols

Professional proofreaders use special marks for punctuation marks and certain symbols (see Appendix B). You do not usually have to know these special marks. Just make your marks clear and conspicuous.

Adding or Replacing by the General Rule

You can add or replace many punctuation marks or symbols the same way you would a letter of the alphabet:

Adding punctuation:

How forcible are right words—*Job 6:25*

Replacing punctuation:

How forcible are right words—*Job 6:25*

Correcting Punctuation Marks in Place

Pointers and Checkmarks. Sometimes the clearest way to add or replace a punctuation mark or symbol is to write it in place. If you do this, flag the mark with a pointer beneath it. It may be wise also to make a checkmark in the margin, so the mark won't be overlooked:

How farcical are wrong words—*Anon* ✓

Periods. If you add a period (either in place or above the line), call attention to it with a pointer. If you replace another character with a period (either in place or above the line), write the period boldly:

Right words enforce and reinforce right deeds—*Anon* ✓

Right words enforce and reinforce right deeds—*Anon* ✓

> ***It takes two to boogie.*** An opening parenthesis needs a closing parenthesis. Brackets, quotation marks, and sometimes dashes belong in pairs. Catch the bachelors.

Commas, Apostrophes, and Quotation Marks. To avoid confusion, commas, apostrophes, and quotation marks should be marked in place—commas below the line, apostrophes and quotation marks above the line.

He said, Yes, thank you is good, but you ✓✓✓✓

cant put it in your pocket. ✓✓

Drawing New Marks over Old

Many punctuation marks can be marked for replacement by carefully drawing the right mark right over the wrong one with a colored pen or pencil. For example, you can change a period to a comma, a semi-colon, a colon, an exclamation point, or a question mark.

. becomes , or ; or : or ! or ?

You must, of course, make it clear that you have marked a change, so flag the mark with a pointer beneath it; it may be wise also to make a checkmark in the margin.

Before marking:

Words in review: Too many, too few; muddled, true.

After marking:

Words in review: Too many, too few; muddled, true? ✓

Marks for Punctuation and Symbols

	Marks	Example	Corrected Copy
Add by the general rule	Pointer in text, punctuation mark or symbol above line	12:01 P.M.	12:01 P.M.
Add by marking in place	Punctuation mark or symbol in place, pointer below line, checkmark in margin	12:01 P.M. ✓	12:01 P.M.
Replace by the general rule	Slash in text, replacement above line,	12:01 P.M.	12:01 P.M.
Replace by drawing over old	Draw new over old in text, checkmark in margin	12:01 P.M. ✓	12:01 P.M.

▶Tips on Checkmarks and Message Rings

- Use the message ring for symbols that could be confused—for example, enclosures (also called fences) such as parentheses, brackets, or braces (curly brackets):

    bonjour(good day) (parens) [ ]

    the impenetrable beaurucracy (sic) (brackets)

    Betty
    Betsy } Elizabeth (brace)
    Bess

- Use checkmarks in the margin whenever it seems sensible—for example, to call attention to an inconspicuous mark:

    Easy come, easy go. ✓

- Use checkmarks, one for each change, to help keep track of the number of corrections in a line:

    Dont say "ouch" if youre not hurt. ✓✓✓✓

- When there's room on a line, you can write the correct words or symbols in place, instead of above the line, and then make a checkmark in the margin:

    A rose by any other name would smell *as sweet.* ✓

- Two of the cornerstones of the Practical Proofreading system are the message ring and the checkmark. Use them freely.

Marks for Hyphens and Dashes

Symbol	To Add	To Replace	Corrected Copy
- hyphen	in‿laws	in‑/laws	in-laws
--dash, typed (2 hyphens)	Yes ‿ and no	Yes/ and no	Yes--and no
—dash, typeset (em dash)	Yes and no (dash)	Yes‑and no (dash)	Yes—and no

Confusing Characters

Confusion with Hyphens and Dashes

Hyphens and dashes can be a source of confusion to people unfamiliar with typeset characters. In typewriter style, two hyphens with no space before or after them usually represent the common dash. In typeset style, hyphens and dashes are separate characters.

Typed hyphen and dash:

```
My great-grandfather--rest his soul--had 10 sons.
```

Typeset hyphen and dash:

My great-grandfather—rest his soul—had 10 sons.

In typeset style, the common dash is an *em* dash—a dash that is one em long. Ems are units of printers' measure. Ems and other kinds of dashes are discussed in Chapter 14.

Note: Although most typists type two hyphens with no spaces before or after them to represent dashes, others add space or use only one hyphen. If you are proofreading copy in typewriter style, be sure dashes are all the same in a single document.

```
Words have wings--and fly away.
Words have wings -- and fly away.
Words have wings - and fly away.
```

Confusion with Quotation Marks and Apostrophes

In typewriter style, foot marks (') and inch marks (") represent apostrophes and quotation marks. Because they are straight up and down, these symbols serve as both opening and closing quotation marks. In typeset style, true quotation marks are curly (" ") or, in some type-faces, weighted (" "), and opening marks differ from closing marks.

Typewriter style: "He's 6'2" tall and a yard wide."

Typeset style: "He's 6'2" tall and a yard wide."

In any typographic style, many people are confused about the use of apostrophes. Here is a brief review of their two purposes:

Apostrophes represent omitted characters in contractions. They belong where the missing letters or numbers would go: can't = cannot; there's = there is; 'twas = it was; '49ers = 1849ers; it's = it is.

Apostrophes indicate possession. One way to figure out where most possessive apostrophes go is to turn the phrase around in your mind and put the apostrophe after the word that ends the turned-around phrase.[1] For example, when you turn *the officers' conference* around to *the conference of the officers,* you see that the apostrophe belongs after the *s* in *officers.* Turn *men's clothing* around to *clothing of the men,* and you see that the apostrophe goes after the *n* in *men.* Turn *the treasurer's report* around to *the report of the treasurer* to see that the apostrophe goes after the last *r* in *treasurer.*

Apostrophes do *not* belong in possessive pronouns (such as *hers, ours, theirs,* or *its*), and when they appear there they need to be corrected. Watch for "it's" where "its" belongs; this is a common error:

Virtue is it̸s own reward.

> ***Don't use buckshot when one bullet will do.*** Recurring errors may need only a general note instead of a mark at each instance. If, however, you're not sure that a widespread error can be universally corrected (for example, with one search-and-replace command on a computer), first, write a general note explaining the problem; then, make a checkmark in the margin at each occurrence.

---

[1] Some style guides give more complicated rules, but this method usually provides acceptable punctuation.

Tips on Marking for Punctuation Marks and Symbols

Quotation Marks and Apostrophes

■ Be sure to exaggerate the curves when you mark for true quotation marks or apostrophes:

 *(curly apos & quotes)* Don't say "ouch" if you're not hurt.

■ Watch for opening single quotation marks (') mistakenly used instead of apostrophes (') in abbreviations like *'twas* and *'76*.

■ Watch for quotation marks that face the wrong way.

■ Watch for foot and inch marks wrongly used when true quotation marks are available. Watch also for the problem in reverse—quotation marks used for inch or foot marks:

(Set inch marks)
16" TV for Sale

Commas and Periods

■ Headings that are set apart on a page do not need periods.

Chapter 100.

■ In the United States, nearly every style guide calls for commas and periods to go inside closing quotation marks.[2]

She said, "Thanks," and I said, "You're welcome."

The American style guides that call for periods and commas inside closing quotation marks vary slightly in specifying what happens to other punctuation, but other marks usually go inside quotation marks only if they are part of the quotation.

She said, "Thanks"; he said, "I thank you, too"; and I said, "O.K."

---

[2] The reason is aesthetic: they look better there. A few technical style guides have adopted the British tradition, which is logical rather than typographically attractive and which places any punctuation outside quotation marks unless it is part of what's quoted.

More Tips on Marking for Punctuation Marks and Symbols

■ Commas should set off the elements of place names (such as the name of a city from that of a state or country) and the elements of dates. Watch for omission of the final comma, a common error:

✓   Chicago, Illinois‚is the largest city in the state but not the capital.   ^

   There are as many traffic problems in Bangkok, Thailand‚ ✓ as in New York City.   ^

   On Sunday, December 7, 1941‚Pearl Harbor was attacked. ✓   ^

Note: No comma is needed when just the month and year appear (December 1941 was the month Pearl Harbor was attacked) or when the date is given in military style (On 7 December 1941 Pearl Harbor was attacked).

Parentheses, Fractions, and Other Characters

■ Watch for periods or other terminal punctuation misplaced with closing parentheses, a common error. If the words in parentheses are part of the sentence, the period belongs outside the parentheses. If the words in parentheses are *not* part of the sentence, a period belongs at the end of the sentence and, usually, another at the end of the words inside the parentheses.

 – Terminal punctuation goes outside parentheses that are part of a sentence (like this).

 – Terminal punctuation goes inside separate parentheses. (This is an example.)

■ In typewriter style, a hyphen is usually typed between a whole number and a fraction: 2-1/4. In typeset copy, fractions should be set like this: 2¼.

   ½ *set proper fraction*

   The standard size for bond paper is 8 1/2 by 11 inches.

■ Computers and word processors make available a great variety of typefaces, sizes, styles, and characters. If it's possible and desirable for the material you proofread to be set in the more traditional characters—true dashes, quotation marks, or fractions, for example—mark for the change in a message ring.

Practice 10. Marks for Punctuation and Symbols

Instructions: Mark to add or replace punctuation marks and symbols. Use text marks. Compare your work with the answer key in Appendix C.

A. Missing Punctuation and Symbols

1. One inch equals 2.54 centimeters

2. The program begins at 730 p.m.

3. For sale: table, $20; 4 chairs, $10 each, corner cupboard, $30.

4. Waste not want not.

5. The door of success is marked with two words, "Push and "Pull.

6. $2^2 = 4$, $4^2 = 16$, $16 = 256$.

7. We have not heard from you since we shipped your last order on February 28, 1995 to London, Ontario in care of Mr. F. Galway. May we send our new price list.

B. Typewriter-Style Hyphens and Dashes

Mark for hyphens and dashes in typewriter style.

```
In belllike tones, the exgovernor--the twenty
first to hold office, announced the formation of
a semiindependent agency to aid the self
employed.
```

C. Typeset-Style Hyphens and Dashes

Mark for hyphens and dashes in copy to be typeset.

In belllike tones, the exgovernor--the twenty first to hold office, announced the formation of a semiindependent agency to aid the self employed.

Practice 11. Review of Marks (Direct Proofreading)

Instructions: Mark the following for correction. Use text marks. Assume that the quotations and their citations are accurate except for obvious misspellings. Compare your work with the answer key in Appendix C.

Why New Proofreaders Suffer form Despondency

When you fist read proof you learn to your horror that you can miss, that perfection is an unreachable gaol

Next, you learn that even when your work is perfect, not all the errors you caught will be corrected; that even when corrections are made they aren't always done right; and that ever when it was done right, new errors can occur. In fact, new errors can occur at any stage of production for many reasons beside human error, including faulty equipment (for example, interrupted electronic operation (resulting, for example, in garble.)

Last, the hardest lesson leaned is this: Others may be allowed to be imperfect, but proofreaders are not. Perfection, it seems, is a proofreaders' duty.

The professionals in the publications business have known about this altitude for a long time.

Theodore Low De Vinne,[1] a distinguished typograper and type designer at the turn of the century, wrote, "The proofreader's position is not an enviable one....He may correct ninety-nine errors out of a hunderd, but if he misses the hundredth he may be sharply reproved."

Benjamin Drew,[1] printer, scholar, teacher, and proofreader at the Cambridge University Press and than at the United States Goverment Printing Office gives us this good advice: "Let no nervous or touchy man meddle with proofreading".

---

1. Quted from *The Practice of Typography, Correct Composition* by Theodore Low De Vinne, Oswald Publishig Company, N.Y., 1902.

2. Quoted from *Pens an Types* by Benjamin Drew, Lee and Shepard, Boston, 1889.

Practice 12. Review of Marks (Comparison Proofreading)

Instructions: Mark the column on the right to match the column on the left. Use text marks. Compare your marks with the answer key in Appendix C.

Views on Error

Inland Printer (1887): Errors ... intrude themselves in the most preposterous manner, when and where they are not wanted, turn sense into nonsense, and upset the wisdom of the lawmakers and the devotion of the saints.

Dryden: Errors, like straws, upon the surface flow; He who would search for pearls must dive below.

Marilyn Vos Savant: While no one has yet figured out a way to eliminate human error, we always do the next best thing. We correct ourselves.

Sophocles: He who is not too stubborn to heal the ills his errors caused shows wisdom and earns blessings.

James Joyce: A man of genius makes no mistakes. His errors are volitional and are the portals of discovery.

Anon: The longer a man is wrong, the surer he is that he's right.

G.K. Chesterton: An error is more menacing than a crime, for an error begets crime.

Views of Error

Inland Printer (1887). Errors ... intrude themselves in the most preposterous manner when and where they are not wanted, turn sense ito non-sense, and upset the wisdom of the lawmakers and demotion of the saints.

Dryden: Errors, like straws, upon the surface flow; He who would search for pearls must dive low.

Marilyn Vos Savant: While no one has yet figured cut a way to eliminate human error, we do always the next best thing. We correct ourself

Sophocles: He who is too stubborn to heel the ills caused by his errors shows wisdom and earns blessing.

James Joyce: A man of genius makes no mistakes at all. His errors are the portals of discovery.

G.K. Chesterton: An error is more menacing than a crime for error begets crime.

Practice 13. More Blatant Errors in Grammar and Usage

Instructions: Correct the errors, including nonstandard grammar and usage. Compare your work with the answer key in Appendix C. For a list of further resources on grammar and punctuation, see Appendix A.

1. I smelled something burning, so I look around and I seen smoke coming from the oven.

2. She don't know which of the files might could be theirs'.

3. I hunted for the information everywheres I could think of, but I don't know where its at.

4. I take my "breaks" in the smoking area like a cigarette smoker should.

5. When you take a message on the phone, you had ought to ask this question "Whom may I say is calling"?

6. The sales' force exceeded it's goals and which was commendable.

7. My teacher didnt learn me nothing about possessive apostrophes, so please tell me when I'm mistakened.

8. Dear Mr. Soenso,

   This is the second reminder from us about invoice number 9991 for $650.98 and invoice number 9991A for $1.29, their both of which comes to $652.27 and which is now more than 90 days' overdo. We are sending this letter by certified mail, return receipt requested to be sure you recieve it. Please get in touch with me right away so we can straighten this out. We've got some sensational products coming up and we would'nt want you to loose out.

   Hopeing for your promp response.

   Sincerely

   Parker Plaice

   Account Represemtative

8. Marking for Type Style Changes

Chapter 8

Marking for Type Style Changes

How to Mark for Changes in Type Style

When the characters in the text are the right ones but the type style is wrong, it's a good idea to mark with margin marks even when there is plenty of space between lines. Here's how:

1. Mark a ring in the text around characters with the wrong type style.

2. Write instructions in a ring in the margin.

  words are what distinguish the Human animal. (lc)

In one line or one passage, a single message ring can account for several text rings by specifying how many times the same change needs doing. (Use the times sign: 2 ×, 3 ×, and so on.)

Margin Mark	Text Mark	Corrected Copy
lc 2×	LETTER PERFECT	Letter Perfect

Another way to solve the same problem is to ring both words and mark for caps and lowercase (Clc):

Margin Mark	Text Mark	Corrected Copy
Clc	LETTER PERFECT	Letter Perfect

You can ring a word, several words, a group of characters, or several lines and mark for all lowercase or all capitals even though some of the characters are already lowercased or capitalized:

Margin Mark	Text Mark	Corrected Copy
all caps	Alicia Koke) What	ALICIA KOKE: What
all lc	Can Be as Wild as Words?	can be as wild as words?

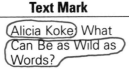

When you change horses in midstream, you can get wet. It's easy to overlook an error set in a different typeface from the text face you are reading. Watch out when type changes to all caps, italics, boldface, small sizes, and large sizes. Watch out when underlines appear in typewritten copy.

If you prefer, you can mark individual letters for lowercase by simple replacement so long as you don't print but write carefully in cursive script:

To get this: Be careful out there!

Do this: Be Careful Out There!   *lc 3x*

Or this: Be Careful Out There!   ✓ ✓ ✓

When you mark for lowercase by replacement, the reason to use cursive script instead of hand printing is this: Hand-printed letters can be taken for either capitals or lowercase in about half the alphabet.

For the same reason, take care if you mark for capitals by replacement:

To get this: Be Careful Out There!

Do this: Be careful out there!   *caps 3x*

Not this: Be careful out there!   ✓ ✓ ✓

Marks for Type Style

Specification	Marks Margin	Marks Text	Corrected Copy
Lowercase	lc	Mares eat Oats	Mares eat oats
	lc	DOES EAT OATS	Does eat oats
Italic	ital	Little lambs eat ivy	*Little lambs eat ivy*
Roman[1]	Rom	A kid'll eat ivy, too	A kid'll eat ivy, too
All caps	caps	parrots eat carrots	PARROTS EAT CARROTS
	caps	Apes Eat Grapes	APES EAT GRAPES
Small caps	sc	Goats eat oats	GOATS EAT OATS
Caps and small caps	c&sc	FLIES EAT PIES	FLIES EAT PIES
	c&sc	Bears Eat Berries	BEARS EAT BERRIES
Caps and lowercase	clc	BIG FISH EAT LITTLE FISH	Big Fish Eat Little Fish
	clc	Eat, drink, and be merry	Eat, Drink, and Be Merry
Boldface	BF	It's dog eat dog	**It's dog eat dog**

---

[1] Roman type is defined in Chapter 2 under "Terms to Know Before You Start, Typefaces." "Not ital" is also an acceptable message.

When in doubt about how to mark, use the message ring. For example:

To get this: Be Careful Out There!

Do this: (Be Careful Out There!)   (all rom, caps 3x)

If you prefer, you can mark for italic by underlining type and writing (ital) as the message. In fact, a single underline is the standard type-mark for italic, and in typewriter style, underlines substitute for italic. (Therefore, when italic type is available, underlining is not needed.)

To get this: Good morning *(Bon jour).*

Do this: Good morning (Bon jour).   (ital)

Or this: Good morning (Bon jour).   (ital)

Note: When you mark for type style changes, it's wise to restrict underlining to marking for italic. You risk confusion if you underline for other type style changes (for boldface or caps, for example), because your marks will conflict with the traditional, professional system of typemarking with various kinds of underlines. The ring in the text and the message in the margin are always safe.

The ordinary form of type—not italicized or boldfaced—is called "regular" or "plain text" or sometimes "lightface (LF)." Mark a message with these terms only if you're sure the person making corrections will understand. Writing "not bold" or "not ital" may be safer.

Margin Mark	Text Mark	Corrected Copy
(Not bold)	(**It's dog eat dog.**)	It's dog eat dog.

How to Mark for Any Typographic Change

Mark for any typographic change—in case,[2] typeface, type size, or type style—with a ring in text and a message ring in the margin.

Here, for example, is how to mark to change 14-point type to another size:

Margin Mark	Text Mark	Corrected Copy
(18 pt)	(Big words)	Big words

Here's how to mark to change 14-point Times to 13-point Helvetica:

Margin Mark	Text Mark	Corrected Copy
(13 pt Helvetica)	(Words, words, words)	Words, words, words

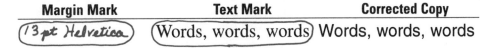

---

[2] "Case" here is used in its typographic sense, referring to uppercase and lowercase, so called because in the days when type was set by hand, the capitals were kept in a type case above the case containing the small letters.

▶ Tips on Marking for Typographic Change

- When you mark for italic or boldface, be sure to consider the punctuation that immediately follows. Include any comma, semicolon, colon, period, dash, hyphen, exclamation point, or question mark (unless, of course, instructed otherwise). Include quotation marks and parentheses only when it makes sense to include both the opening and closing marks. (See the examples above.)

- Be sure the people working from your marks understand how roman, italic, and boldface forms of type differ and know the meaning of abbreviations like "ital" and "rom." Give them a copy of the page that appears on the inside back cover of this book.

- In comparison proofreading, watch carefully for mistakes in style choices. It's not always easy to catch errors, because the format of the new copy usually differs from the old, and you may be comparing different typefaces, type sizes, and spacing details, including line length.

- Some complex problems may be more clearly marked with a message ring above the line (when there is enough space there). For example, when words are to be moved to a new place in the line, margin marks for changing type style could be confusing:

  Leash dogs when visitors come, unless they are well behaved.

- Some people use kite strings (guidelines) to connect the marks in the text with those in the margin. Kite strings, however, can be untidy and, when there are many, confusing. For most copy requiring margin marks, you should use separate marks in the line and the margin. But use kite strings where it's sensible—for example, in wide tables, spreadsheets with many tightly set columns, or illustrations with scattered labels. Kite strings look like this:

  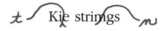

Practice 14. Changing Type Style

Instructions: Mark the column on the right to match the column on the left. Ignore the differences due to the new typeface (a new version often differs from an old in typeface or spacing or both). Use text marks. Compare your work with the answer key in Appendix C.

Words About Words

A powerful agent is the right word.
—*Mark Twain*

Longer than deeds liveth the word.
—*Pindar*

Be not the slave of words.
—*Carlyle*

Words are stubborn.   —*Zartman*

Words make love.
—*André Breton*

A word, once sent abroad, flies irrevocably.   —*Horace*

People who say they love words are the biggest bores of all.
—*Minor*

Words pay no debts.
—*Shakespeare*

Syllables govern the world.
—*John Selden*

Words purr, words roar; words stir, words bore.   —*Mateus*

Actions speak louder than words. A picture is worth a thousand words.   —*Old Proverbs*

What masters of the language know: Big words sputter; little ones glow.   —*Timothy Rufus*

Many a legal case or public question is settled by getting the words right.   —*J.S. Schultz*

Words about Words

A powerful agent is the right word.
—Mark Twain

Longer than deeds liveth the word.
—*PINDAR*

Be not the slave of words.   —*Carlyle*

Words are stubborn.   —*Zartman*

Words make love.   **André Breton**

A Word, Once Sent Abroad, flies irrevocably.   —*Horace*

People who say they love words are *the* biggest bores of all.   —*Minor*

Words pay no debts.   —*ShakeSpeare*

SYLLABLES govern the world.
—*John Selden*

Words purr, words roar; words stir, words bore.   —*mateus*

Actions speak louder than words. A picture is worth a thousand words.
—*Old proverbs*

What masters of the language *know:* big words sputter; Little ones glow.
—*Timothy Rufus*

Many a legal case or public question is settled by getting the words right.
—*J.S. Schultz*

Rules for Margin Marks

Messages in the margin, which follow the rules for margin marks, are practical for most type style changes because margins provide space for clear, conspicuous messages. Margin marks are essential for any kind of correction on copy that is tightly spaced.

Margin marks differ from text marks in the ways prescribed by these rules:

Rule 1. Make Sure Every Mark in the Text Corresponds with a Mark or Message in the Margin

(cap)　ⓜark in pairs, text and margin.

For adding, taking out, and replacing characters, mark in the margin what would go above the line if there were room. For transposition, mark a double loop in the text and a checkmark in the margin. For a change in type style, ring the characters in the text and write the instruction in a message ring in the margin.

Rule 2. Mark in the Margin Nearer to the Text Mark

You need not be precise about dividing the page down the middle to make marks at the left and right. Just use both margins as best you can.

(cap)　ⓜark in the nearer Ⓜargin.　　(lc)

Rule 3. Mark in the Margin from Left to Right, Separating Marks with Slashes

k/ɣ Mar from left to ɡ right ~~write~~ slashes betweeⓔ marks.　*with/✓*

The Different Margin Marks

Correction	Mark in Text	Mark in Margin	Example	
Add	pointer	character(s) to add	ad͟dition	*d*
Take out	slash or strike-through	take-out loop	take /out	*ɣ*
Replace	slash or strike-through	correct character(s)	rep͟lacement	*a*
Transpose	double loop	checkmark	ta͡nsposition	*✓*
Change type style	ring	message ring	Ⓛowercase	*(lc)*

Examples of Margin Marks

The copy on the right has been compared with that on the left, and
the corrections marked in the spaces representing the margins:

TWINKLE, TWINKLE, little star!   Twinkle, Twinkle, little ~~bat~~!   *star*

How I wonder what you are!   How I wonder hat you're at!   *wˆ/are*

Up above the world so high,   ✓ Up above the wrold ~~you fly~~,   *so high*

Like a diamond in the sky. *diamond* Like a ~~teatray~~ in the sky./   *&*

—Jane Taylor   —Lewis Carroll   *Jane Taylor*

Practice 15. Using Margin Marks (Comparison Proofreading)

Instructions: Compare the old version on the left with the new version on the right, and mark the errors in the new according to the rules for margin marks. Use the space between the two versions as the left-hand margin. Compare your work with the answer key in Appendix C.

Sentences A to Z

Each of the following sentences contains every letter of the alphabet.

- A quick brown fox jumps over the lazy dog.

- Pack my box with five dozen liquor jugs.

- Quick wafting zephyrs vex bold Jim.

- The fox, jaw bleeding, moved quickly to daze his prey.

- Why did Max become elo-quent over a zany gift like jodhpurs?

- Brown jars prevented the mix-ture from freezing too quickly.

- The bank recognizes the claim as valid and quite just, and we expect full payment.

- Judge Power quickly gave the sixty embezzlers stiff sentences.

- Zoe ma grand fille veut que je boive ce whisky dont je ne veux pas.

- Kaufen Sie jede Woche vier gute bequeme Pelze xy.

Sentences A to Z

Each of the folllowing sentences contains every letter of the alphabet.

- A quick brown fox jumped over the lazy hog.

- Pack my box with four dozen liguor jugs.

- Quick wafting zephrs vex bald Jim.

- The fox, jaw bleeding, moved quickly to daze his pray.

- Why did Max become elo-quent over a zany gift like jodphurs?

- Brown jars prevented the mix-ture from freezing too quickly

- The bank recognizes the clam as valid and quite just, and we expect full payment.

- Judge Power quickly gave the six embezzlers stiff sentences.

- Zoe ma grand fille veut que je boive ce whisky dont je ne ne veux pas.

- Kaufen Sie jede woche vien gute bequeme Pelze xy.

Practice 16. Still More Blatant Errors in Grammar and Usage

A. Danglers

Instructions: Use text marks to correct all errors. Instead of rewriting, rearrange the parts of the following sentences. Use double curves or brackets and arrows. Mark punctuation, caps, and lowercase to suit the changes. Compare your work with the answer key in Appendix C.
Example:

Grilled in foil, those who shy away from onions may like the vegetables.

1. Your invitation come when I was busy moving my office and was mislaid.

2. He had a cough when he went to school along with a lot of other symptoms.

3. The new movie, "Dracula" terrifies everyone now showing at theaters.

4. The 36-inch telescope will be use in a systematic search for supernovas designed by astrophysicists from Berkeley.

5. Hidden in the dining room breakfront in a box enameled with blue flowers, Mary Michael keeps the keys to 15 neighbor's houses.

B. Problems with Sentence Structure

Instructions: Use text marks to correct problems.

1. I don't want nobody working after five o'clock. The funds budgeted for overtime having run out.

2. Don't waste motion. Work like I do. With no extra effort. Just enough to do the job.

3. Dear Parker Plaice:

You have written me two letters saying that I owe you money and you are mistaken, on September 1, the day I received the goods from you I wrote check number 325 on the First Commercial Bank and Trust Co. for $652.27 and mailed it, you cashed it, it came back to me with my bank statement for October, it is in my files. Please check your records, if it will help resolve the problem I will get a copy made of the check and send it to you.

Sincerely yours,

George T Soenso

9. Adding and Taking Out Space

Chapter 9

Adding and Taking Out Space

How to Mark with Close-up Hooks

Taking Out All Extra Space Between Characters

As you know, double close-up hooks (⌇) show whether added characters should be connected at their left or their right:

Close-up hooks connect added characters at their lef⌄ or their ⌄ight.

These double close-up hooks have another purpose. Use them to mark to take out all extra space and change two words or character groupings to one:

Proofreading is a pain⌒staking process.

Reducing Space Between Words

Use a single hook (⌒) to take out some but not all extra space between words in a line—that is, to close up part way:

Distance ⌒ makes the heart grow fonder.

How to Mark with the Space Sign

The symbol # stands for the word "space." This useful symbol is standard typographer's shorthand, although its specialized meaning is new to many people. It's easy to get used to, however. When you use it, be sure that everyone who works with your marks understands what the symbol means.

> ***Every yoo-hoo deserves a yoo-hoo back.*** A footnote reference calls out for the footnote; a first reference to a table or an illustration calls out for the table or illustration. Be sure a footnote begins on the same page or column as its callout. Be sure a table or illustration follows its callout as soon as possible.

Marks for Adding and Taking Out Space

Symbol	Meaning	Example	Corrected Copy
Space sign and pointer	Add space between words or characters	spaceneeded	space needed
Space sign and pointer	Add space between lines	abcdefghi jklmnopqr stuvwxyz	abcdefghi jklmnopqr stuvwxyz
Space sign and extended pointer	Add space between columns	abc def ghi jkl mno pqr stu vwx yz	abc def ghi jkl mno pqr stu vwx yz
Double close-up hooks	Take out all space; make one word	word	word
Single hook	Take out some space; close up part way	less space	iess space
Hook and message	Take out space between lines	abcdefghi jklmnopqr *less #* stuvwxyz	abcdefghi jklmnopqr stuvwxyz
Hook and message	Take out space between columns	abc def *less #* ghi jkl mno pqr stu vwx yz	abc def ghi jkl mno pqr stu vwx yz

Adding Space Between Lines or Columns

These are the guidelines for marking for added space:

1. Mark the spot needing added space so there's no mistaking it.

2. Label the spot so that what needs to be done is clear.

A good way to mark the spot needing space is to use a pointer (> or ∧), extending it if needed, and a good way to keep the instruction simple is to use the space sign (#).

- To mark for added space between lines:

> You can't put more soup in the bowl than you have in the pot.
You can't pick more apples than you have in the tree.

You can't drink more wine than you have in the bottle.

■ To mark for added space between columns:

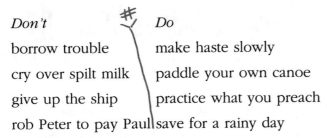

Don't	*Do*
borrow trouble	make haste slowly
cry over spilt milk	paddle your own canoe
give up the ship	practice what you preach
rob Peter to pay Paul	save for a rainy day

■ To mark for added space between words:

Two heads are better than one.

Reducing Space Between Lines or Columns

These are the guidelines to mark for less space between lines or columns:

1. Mark the spot needing less space so there's no mistaking it.

2. Label the spot so that what needs to be done is clear.

A good way to mark the spot needing reduced space is with a single hook, meaning close up part way, and a good way to keep the instruction simple is to write *(less #)* in a message ring.

■ To mark for less space between lines:

You can't put more soup in the bowl than you have in the pot.

You can't pick more apples than you have in the tree.

(less #) You can't drink more wine than you have in the bottle.

■ To mark for less space between columns:

Don't	*(less #)*	*Do*
borrow trouble		make haste slowly
cry over spilt milk		paddle your own canoe
give up the ship		practice what you preach
rob Peter to pay Paul		save for a rainy day

► Tips on Marking to Change Spacing

- In proofreading, **#** means "space." When marking, do not use this symbol to mean anything else. But if you want the symbol itself to be typed or typeset (as a number sign or a sharp sign, for example), ask for it with a message ring:

Mark	Corrected Copy
(number sign) #1, #2, 3, #4, #5	#1, #2, #3, #4, #5
(sharp sign) Prelude in C Minor	Prelude in C# Minor

- If you proofread a form to be filled out in handwriting, be sure the blank lines are not too crowded:

Yes! Please send me your free sample.

NAME_____

ADDRESS_____ < #

CITY_____STATE____ZIP_____ < #

- You can use the space sign to mark to replace a character with space (the same idea as erasing a character and leaving blank the space it used to occupy):

#

Swingslow, sweet chariot.

- Replacement is usually the easiest solution to complex problems involving type and spacing:

Too complicated:

Again and gain the optimists have called the loss gain.

Better:

Again and gain the optimists have called the loss gain.

Too complicated:

Better late thanever.

Better:

Better late thanever.

▶ More Tips on Marking to Change Spacing

- In any document, the quality of the spacing largely determines the quality of the typography.

  Equal word spacing (the space between words) and even line spacing (the space between lines) are characteristics of good typographic quality.

  Word spacing in ragged-right copy (set with an uneven right margin) differs from that in justified copy (set with even margins at left and right).

  Examples of justified and ragged-right copy:

  This is an example of justified copy set in a narrow line measure. Left and right margins are even, but word spacing varies from line to line. Hyphens at end-of-line word breaks help keep word spacing reasonably regular.

  Justified copy

  This is an example of copy with a ragged-right margin set in narrow line measure. The left margin is even. The word spacing is regular. For some copy, hyphens at end-of-line word breaks can help make the right margin less ragged.

  Ragged-right copy

  In justified typeset copy with proportionally spaced characters, word spacing varies slightly from line to line, but it should look the same from word to word within any one line. Unequal word spacing in a typeset line needs to be corrected.

  In justified typewriter-style copy, where characters are mono-spaced, equal word spacing is not possible.

  Make sure line spacing is equal in any typeset unit such as a paragraph. In word processing or desktop publishing, for example, watch for unequal line spacing after a large initial cap:

  Make sure line spacing is equal
  in any unit such as a paragraph.
  Watch especially for unequal line
  spacing after a large initial cap.

▶ More Tips on Marking to Change Spacing

- "Lakes"—wide spaces between words—and "rivers of white"—irregular streams of white space through the text—may occur in justified material with short lines. Here are examples:

> Watch for "lakes" and "rivers," that is, irregular streams of space through a passage of type, especially in justified material set with short lines.

- If you need greater precision in marking between words, you can extend the line of a pointer; between lines or columns, you can do the same or you can draw an arrow:

 You can't drink more wine than you have in the bottle.

You can't pick more apples

than you have in the tree.

You can't drink more wine than you have in the bottle.

You can't pick more apples

than you have in the tree.

- When you use both text marks and margin marks, use checkmarks to count the number of corrections to be made in a line.

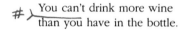 What do you mean, <u>bon soir</u>? It's no on! ✓✓

Differing Spacing Conventions

Standard, monospaced typewriter style in the United States calls for one space between words and two spaces after the punctuation ending a sentence (or after a colon). This standard is changing, however, because typesetting with proportionally spaced characters requires the same space between sentences as between words. For this reason, word processed copy prepared for conversion to typesetting should be typed with only one stroke of the space key after any group of characters—a word by itself or a word followed by punctuation.

If you follow the typewriter convention, one space after a sentence needs to be marked for added space with a pointer and a space sign:

```
       A sentence can be declarative, interrogative,
       imperative, or exclamatory.  Sometimes the same
       thought can be expressed all four ways: I need
  #    your help. Will you help me?  Help me with this.
       Help!
```

If you follow the typesetting convention, two spaces after a sentence need to be marked for less space with a single hook and perhaps a checkmark in the margin:

```
       A sentence can be declarative, interrogative, imperative, or
       exclamatory. Sometimes the same thought can be expressed all
       four ways: I need your help. Will you help me? Help me with
       this. Help!
```

The standard indention for paragraphs differs in typeset copy from typewriter-style copy,[1] but all you need to check is that indention is consistent in any one document.

---

[1] The standard paragraph indent for typeset copy is one em; for typewriter copy, five spaces. See Chapter 14 for an explanation of ems.

Practice 17. Adding and Taking Out Space

Instructions: Use text marks. For spacing errors, use the space or close-up marks when practical; otherwise mark for replacement or use a message ring. For other errors, mark as usual. Compare your work with the answer key in Appendix C.

A. One Word or Two

Mark the column on the right to match the column on the left.

around	a round
be long	belong
ground cover	groundscover
a ward	award
vanguard	van guard
cardboard	carddboard
in exact position	inexact position

B. Sentences

Mark to change spacing in sentences 1 through 4 so they make better sense. Mark sentence 5 for three missing letter *a*'s as well as for spacing errors.

1. The product often thousand times zero is zero.

2. We hope for better grow thin our low-calorie milkshake.

3. Proofreaders need many qualities; noon equality is most important.

4. We bough there very thing she wanted.

5. She was incross mood because she had comecross crossword puzzle she couldn't finish.

C. Paragraph

Mark all errors.

EVERY ONE who works with paper—and that includes

those who's work involves gift rap, wallpaper, male, or any

kind of document—should follow   this advise: Never shear

your work surface with aliquid that can spill. Experienced

proofreaders can tell many an antidote about soggy proof

sheets or dripping manuscripts caused by care less people
ignoring that sample rule.

10. Changes in Position or Placement

Chapter 10

Changes in Position or Placement

How to Mark Paragraph Breaks

The symbol ¶ stands for "paragraph." Use it to show where a paragraph break begins:

> Write legibly. Bad handwriting is as insulting as whispering with your mouth full and your head turned away. ¶Write simply. Use plain words, courteous and hospitable. Show me your orderly mind and your generous spirit.

Use the message (no ¶) to show where a paragraph break is wrong:

> Write legibly. Bad handwriting is as insulting as whispering with your mouth full and your head turned away.
> Write simply. Use plain words, courteous and hospitable.
> (No ¶) Show me your orderly mind and your generous spirit.

How to Mark Word Breaks

When a word of more than one syllable will not fit at the end of a line, it can be divided with a hyphen. To make reading easy, words should be divided at the end of a syllable, preferably so that the first part gives a clue to what the whole word is. However, even the best word-dividing computer program will sometimes create unacceptable word divisions.

Use a standard dictionary or word-division guide to look up where hyphens should divide words at the ends of lines. (Stay with the same reference; authorities differ.)

Marks for Changes in Position or Placement

	Instruction	Example
Paragraph break	Mark pointer in text and paragraph sign above line or in margin.	"Who goes there?" "A friend."
Word break	Strike through bad break, and write word with correct break in margin.	~~Proofr eading~~ *Proof-reading*
	OR	
	Strike through bad break, show all correct breaks in margin, and write message "Choose break."	~~Proofr eading~~ *Proof-read-ing* (Choose break)
Bad line breaks, misalignment, needed repositioning, widows, rivers, unequal word or line space, and other spacing or positioning problems	1. Use lines, brackets, arrows, or outline to mark exact spot(s) needing correction. 2. In message ring, describe problem or what needs to be done.	A misprint kills a sensitive author. An intentional change of his text murders him. (merge lines) No wonder so many poets die young. —Oliver W. Holmes

When you find a wrong word division, replace the entire word: Cross out both parts of the word in the text, and write out the word in the margin with a hyphen at the correct breaking point:

.........~~Proofr eading~~......... *Proof-reading*

Moving letters down to the next line, as shown above, is almost always the way to correct a bad word division. If, however, you can't tell where the best break is, you can show hyphens at all the correct breaks—along with a message to the corrector so there will be no misunderstanding:

......A proofreader is a harsh ~~disciplina- rian~~......... *dis-ci-pli-nar-i-an* (choose break)

Here are two of the main *don'ts* of word division:[1]

- Don't divide one-syllable words—for example, before *ed* in "launched."

- Don't separate one letter from the rest of a word. A hyphen does not belong before or after a one-letter syllable. For example, write out the word "imaginary" as *imagi-nary* or *imag-inary*; division would be incorrect after the one-letter first syllable *(i-)* or before the one-letter last syllable *(-y)*.

You should mark for correction when hyphens appear at the ends of more than three consecutive lines; some authorities permit only two.

Long-standing typographic prin-
ciples assert that ladders of hyphens (three or four) are not per-
mitted because they spoil the ap-
pearance of a page.

4 hyphens

How to Mark Bad Line Breaks, Misalignment, and Other Problems

Marks for repositioning or changing the placement of type should be obvious; for example, a straight line can show where to straighten misaligned type, or a bracket and an arrow can show where to move a misplaced block of type.

Examples of such marks follow, but you can mark most problems involving the moving of type clearly and correctly in other ways than the ones shown. Use your common sense. The object, as in all Practical Proofreading, is to catch the problems and mark them so whoever makes the corrections understands what to do.

Bad Line Breaks

- To move words down to the next line:

    Words are like autumn leaves, (And where   Break
    they most abound
    Much fruit of sense beneath
    Is rarely found.

- To move words back to the previous line:

    Words are like autumn
     leaves, And where they most abound
    Much fruit of sense beneath
    Is rarely found.

---

[1] A more detailed list appears in Chapter 12.

■ To merge lines:

Words are like
autumn leaves,
And where they most abound
Much fruit of sense beneath
Is rarely found.

no break

Repositioning

■ To move a line or block of type to a new position on the same page:

Xxxxxxxxxxxxxxxxxxxxxxxxxxxxxxxxxxxxxxxxxxxxxxxxxxxxx
xxxxxxXxxxxxxxxxxxxxxxxxxxxxxxx.xxx
Xxxxxxxxxxxxxxxxxxxxxxxxxxxxxxxxxxxxxxxxxxxxxxxxx
xxxxxxxxxxxxxxxXxxxxxxxxx\xxxxxxxxxxxxxxxxxxxxXxx
xxxxxxxxxxxxxxxxxxxx.
XxxxxxxxxxxxxxxxxxxxxxxxxxxxxxxxxxXxxxxxxxxxxxxxx
xxxxxxxxxxxxxxxxxxxxxxxxxxxxxxxxx.

■ To correct sequence:

③   ②   ①

She seashore by the sells seashells

Put in order

③ beggar man

② poor man

④ thief

① rich man

■ To move a passage from one page to another:

	11

move to p. 34 Xxxxxxxx xx xxxx x xxxx xxx
Xx xxxx xx x xxxxxx xx xxxxx xxxxx
xxxx, xxxx xx xx xxxx xxxxx xxxx x
xxxxx x xxx xx xxxx xxxxx xx
 	
  Xxxxx xx x xxxx xxx x x xx xxxxxxx.
Xxxx x xxx x xxxx xx x xxx xxxx xxxx
xxxx xxxx xxx.
 	
  xxxxxxxxxx Xxx xx xxxxx xxx xx xxx
xx xx xxx xxxx x xxxx x xxxx.	

34	
Xxx xxxxxxxxxxx xxxxx xxxxx xxx xxxx xxxx xxxxxxxx xxxx xx xxx xx *move fr. p11* xxxx xxx xxxx xx. Xxx xxx xxxxxxxxx. Xxx x xxxxxx xx xxx xxx. Xxx Xxxxx xxx xxxx xxxx xxx xxxxxxxxx xxx xxxx xxxx x x xxxxx xxx xxx xxx xxxx xxx xxx xxx xxxxx xxxxxx xxx xxxx xxx xxxxxxxxx xxx xxxx xxxx x x xxxxx xxx xxxxx xx x xxxx xxx xxx	

Source   **Destination**

■ To center a line or block of type:

Marked Copy	Corrected Copy

HEADLINE

Misalignment

■ To align a ragged column or margin:

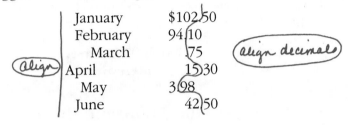

CONTENTS

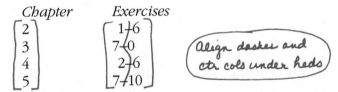

■ To call attention to crooked lines or misaligned words or characters:

If I do not clearly express what I mean, it is either for the rea-

son that, having no conversational powers, I cannot express

what I mean, or that having no meaning, I do not mean what I

fail to express.

—Mr. Grewgious

The Mystery of Edwin Drood

Charles Dickens

■ To move a line or block of type left or right:

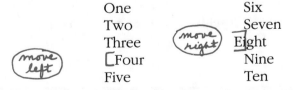

One	Six
Two	Seven
Three	Eight
Four	Nine
Five	Ten

■ To move characters up or down:

proof reading   proof reading,

Tips on Marking for Changes in Position or Placement

- To check for flaws in spacing and positioning, turn the page upside down. This approach can help you catch misalignment and uneven spacing simply because it lets you focus only on the type without being distracted by the words.

- Make sure that headlines and titles longer than one line "break for sense":

Noah Webster: A *(Break)*
Memoir

One Thousand Best- *(Break)*
Loved Poems

Twenty Thousand Leagues Under *(Break)*
the Sea

- Watch for widow lines.[2] The right-hand column here shows examples of two kinds of widow—a very short line at the start of a column or page and a very short line at the end of a paragraph, column, or page.

Even small errors in type cause trouble. Fowler's description of what happens when words are misused, e.g., *deplacement* for *misplacement* or *unquiet* for *unrest,* applies to any of the problems to which a writer's work is

(subject) *(fix widow)*
These slips, he wrote, are unimportant when infrequent, but a writer who makes "a second before the first has faded from memory becomes at once... *(suspect.")* *(fix widow)*

Some people find certain widows acceptable. Few people, however, accept a divided word at the end of a paragraph, a right-hand column, or a page.

Let no paragraph end with a word ~~divi-~~   *division* *(Don't break)*
~~sion.~~

---

[2] Some people call certain kinds of widows "orphans," but not everyone agrees on whether an orphan is at the top of a page or the bottom. Use the term the way those you work with use it.

More Tips on Marking for Changes in Position or Placement

- Convention requires a new paragraph for each new quoted speaker:

  "Do you swear to tell the truth, the whole truth, and nothing but the truth?" "I do."

- Even when you need to move large blocks of copy, always keep the pages of computer output in their original sequence, marking them, for example, *Move to p. X* and *Move from p. X*. The reason is this: Efficient correction of computer output requires the operator to match the words on the printout with the words displayed on the computer screen. If you move the printout's pages around, the operator has to hunt for the original page.

- When landscape pages (pages turned sideways) are placed among portrait pages (upright pages—like those in this book), be sure that their tops appear at the left:

Top of page	
Portrait	Landscape

- Some problems are so complicated that there's no point in trying to figure out everything that's wrong:

  Some problems are so complicated that there's no point in trying to figure out everything that's wrong.

Practice 18. Spacing Marks

Instructions: Mark spacing and other errors. Compare your work with the answer key in Appendix C.

A. The Republic of Letters

Mark to correct bad word division.

> As Washingt-
> on Irving wrote,
> "The rep-
> ublic of let-
> ters is the
> most...di-
> scordant of
> all republ-
> ics, anci-
> ent and modern."

B. My Lord the Book

Divide the following poem (by John Kendrick Bangs) into two verses of four lines each:

> A book is an aristocrat; 'Tis pampered—lives in state;
> Stands on a shelf, with naught whereat
> To worry—
> lovely fate!
> Enjoys the best of company; And
> often—ay, 'tis so—
> Like much in aristocracy,
> Its title makes it go.

C. Invisible Writing

Mark the spacing errors and other problems.

Printing should be invisible," wrote Beatrice type." Type, she said, should be a "transparent Warde, that is, "Type well used is invisible as goblet, a conveyor to look through, rather than hide, the vintage of the humam mind."

Writing, too, we say, should be in visible and transparent, i. e. its meaning should be uncluttered and unclouded   by grammatical, rhetorical, or logical misuse.

Words well used are the vintage of the human mind.

Part Three

Increasing Your Know-how

11. How to Go About the Job

Chapter 11

How to Go About the Job

When in Doubt, Query

Proofreading requires you to make a choice whenever you find
an error:

1. Ignore it.

2. Mark it for correction.

3. Query it.

The choices aren't easy. Most writers treasure their words and don't
take correction well. You, the proofreader, have to be quite sure that
what you mark really needs correcting, that you have the authority to
call for the correction, and that it can be done within the deadline and
the budget and by the available personnel and equipment.

When in doubt about which of the three choices to make, querying—
writing questions to the person responsible for the final product, usually the author—may be the way to go.

Before you query, be sure that queries will be welcome. If they are,
be sure that your queries are the *kind* that will be welcome. This is a
matter of experience and judgment. As a broad rule, query only things
that would greatly puzzle a reader or seriously embarrass the author or
the people you work for.

When you find an error important enough to query, either write your
question directly on the copy (if there's room), write it on a self-stick
note, or type it in a memo:

- If you write on the copy, mark the supposed error in the text
  with a ring, a check, or a pointer. Then, in the margin, write a
  brief, courteous question followed by a question mark in a ring.
  The idea is that this simplifies the work of the author, editor, or
  supervisor—the person who reviews your work. If the author

Why query? To
avoid such a predica-
ment as De Vinne
describes:

"The amiable poet
Cowper has put on
record his anger at a
proofreader who had
tried to improve his
poems; he accused
him of 'rash and gra-
tuitous emendation,'
and with being a
'presumptuous
intermeddler.'"

Never assume that all is well. As the saying goes, "ass-u-me makes an ass out of u and me." Read every character, every heading, every page number. On a letter, read the complimentary close and the list of enclosures. Read boilerplate. Don't skip anything.

rejects your query, the entire question can be crossed out. If the author accepts it, only the question mark needs to be crossed out, and the query now becomes a mark for correction.

Our squeegee, with a contoured wood handle that allows long use without muscle strain and a top-quality rubber blade that is not (effected) by oil, benzene, varnish, or lacquer, are the best on the market.

affected (?)
is (?)
(Our squeegee … is)

- If you write on a self-stick note, cite the page, paragraph, and line number, and write the query like a proofreader's correction. The idea is that the person who reviews your work can decide whether to mark the copy for correction and then discard the note.

  p. 2 para 2 line 4: ~~effected~~ affected?
  line 5: ~~are~~ is? "Our squeegee … is"

- If you write a memo, you can present all the queries in columns:

<u>page</u>	<u>para</u>	<u>line</u>	<u>Query</u>
2	2	4:	~~effected~~ affected?
		5:	~~are~~ is? "Our squeegee...is"

Phrase queries diplomatically, or at least make them as straightforward as the examples. Comments like "Bad grammar" or "No No No!" are unwise.

Watch for recurring errors. Some can be ignored; some need a general query or instruction; some need marks at every instance. If you don't have the authority to solve a problem you find again and again, you should probably write a general query instead of marking every instance:

Summer time and summertime: both appear throughout. Which is preferred?

Chapter heads sometimes centered, sometimes not. OK?

Three Things to Know Before You Start

Know the Equipment

A proofreader who doesn't understand how words get into type isn't fully competent. Proofreaders need to understand how type and art are produced and corrected, which means understanding the capabilities and the limitations of the equipment that produces the documents you work on.

For example, it would be a waste of time to mark every instance of certain kinds of error in computer output. The search-and-replace function, with one command, can correct all misspellings of the same name or replace all double hyphens with dashes or all straight quotation marks (inch marks) with curly ones. It's useful to know which problems can be solved by writing a single instruction:

Set curly quotes throughout "Hello," the Martian said—and I fainted. *Set dashes throughout*

Note: The proofreader who writes an instruction like the one shown above must, of course, be certain that when curly quotes are set throughout, no intentional inch marks are turned into quotation marks.

Many levels of capability are available within the range of low to high tech provided by today's equipment. Proofreaders need to know not only how the copy they mark is produced and corrected but what level of typographic refinement is possible. Sophisticated equipment provides much more than dashes, curly quotes, and small caps. Some of the possibilities are described in Chapter 14.

Know the Purpose and Status of the Document

Match the level of work you do to the purpose of the document. An informal memo to the manager across the hall may need nothing more than a quick scan. A contract or a budget may need several two-person proofreadings and checkings. If a deadline threatens, a missing period in a footnote is unimportant.

The status of the document is also significant. In desktop publishing (DTP), for example, you need to know what stage the document you're reading has reached. It's useless to mark a draft for errors in typeface, type size, line spacing, margins, alignment, justification, indents, or hyphenation; formatting is done entirely through a computer program. Do typographic proofreading only after the draft stage, looking for errors the formatter may have made, especially in italics, boldface, superscript, subscript, and word division.

If you read camera-ready copy, you should understand that the camera will not see the page as you do or perhaps as your photocopying machine does. For example, the camera will not detect pale blue marks, cut-in "windows," or white tape.

Know What's Expected of You

Every time you proofread, you should know exactly what's expected of you. Ask questions if you need to:

■ How far does your authority to make changes go?

■ What's the deadline?

■ What other tasks are involved (for example, filling in blanks in text, such as cross-references; fact checking; making a table of contents; alphabetizing a list)?

■ What reference works are acceptable?[1]

Three Proofreading Methods

Working Solo

For a century or more, comparison proofreading done by a team of two people was the standard in most print shops. Today, however, in many shops and offices, most proofreading is only a "cold read" (direct proofreading) or nothing more than checking corrections. The time-honored method of team proofreading is out of style in favor of a more economical method—solo (one-person) proofreading.

Solo comparison proofreading is especially hard because it involves shifting attention from one version to another every few seconds. When you proofread alone, place the two versions side by side. Use a straightedge such as a ruler to follow along in the old version line by line. Use the eraser end of your pencil to follow the new version word by word. Take special care to catch omissions and unwanted repetitions; they are easy to miss when your eyes skip back and forth. It doesn't hurt to read aloud to yourself.

Working with a Partner

Proofreading with a partner is much more accurate than solo proofreading. For this reason, it is still used for documents that must be error-free such as legal documents and financial statements. The usual procedure is for one partner, the copy holder, to read the old version aloud while the other partner, the proofreader, follows the new copy and marks it for correction.

---

[1] See Appendix A for recommended dictionaries, style guides, and other useful reference books.

Reading Aloud. If you are the copy holder, you must read aloud everything you see:

- Every word, spelling out any that could be misspelled (such as proper names)

- Every punctuation mark

- Every paragraph and any other change in spacing

- Every capital letter and any other change in type style, typeface, or type size.

You might work out some signals and shortcuts with your partner, but you must be sure your partner understands everything you do or say and, of course, everything you agree not to say. For example, you might decide to shorten words like comma (to "com") or semicolon (to "sem"). You might decide not to indicate the capital letter that begins a sentence. Many such shortcuts are possible with partners who work together often.

Marking. If you are the partner doing the marking, you have to be good at spelling. You must look not just at words, but at individual characters, or you will miss errors. You must also look at pages as a whole, or you will miss errors in spacing.

Proofreading with a Tape Recorder

Those who do comparison proofreading solo may find it tiring for their eyes to jump back and forth between the two versions. An electronic partner may be a sensible compromise between the accuracy of partner proofreading and the economy of solo proofreading.

The first step in tape proofreading is to read the old version into a tape recorder, using all the techniques of a copy holder who is a familiar partner to the proofreader—spelling out hard words, calling out punctuation marks and typographic changes, and using recognizable shortcuts and abbreviations.

The next step is to listen to the tape while proofreading the new copy. A person who's fast at reading aloud (and at marking while listening to a tape) takes only a little more time than a solo proofreader who doesn't use a tape recorder.

Some publications use tape proofreading for legal or technical copy because they find that it improves accuracy.

Exercise extra caution at these times:

- When you begin a stint of work, even after a brief interruption.

- When you near the end of a stint of work.

- When you write or type omissions, replacements, or queries; they must be error-free. Never forget that you are just as susceptible to error as any other writer.

- When you're preoccupied or agitated.

119

Computer-Assisted Proofreading

Spell Checkers

When a spell check program is turned on, it will catch words it can neither find in its dictionary nor construct from roots, prefixes, and suffixes. It won't catch typos that are words (It won't cat types that are wards). It's a great help, but not a substitute for a human proofreader.

Grammar Checkers or Editing Programs

A grammar checker or editing program flags many errors. Some—such as repeated words, doubled punctuation, missing halves of paired punctuation, and commas outside closing quotes—help proofreading. Some—such as undesirable expressions (*due to the fact that* instead of *because*), long sentences, and passive voice—are outside the province of most proofreaders. If you use such a program, you should customize it to your needs.

File-Comparison Programs

When two versions of the same document have been entered into a computer, a file-comparison program can indicate where they differ.

This technology can be useful to proofreaders or editors who work directly on a computer and need a record of what they've done. (It's also used to produce inexpensive typesetting abroad, especially in shops where the typesetters don't know English. To set type, an operator keys the copy, another operator keys the same copy, and, when the program indicates that the input is different, the second operator decides what's correct.)

Speech Synthesizers

A speech synthesizer can scan copy and read aloud from type or electronic input in a choice of pleasant voices at an adjustable speed. It can be set to read capitals and punctuation and is at least 90 percent accurate. A proofreader can use it as an electronic partner.

Installed in a computer, a speech synthesizer can read aloud from the text that's been entered. Writers may find such a program helpful to catch errors and to listen to the logic and flow of their own work. Typists may find it increases accuracy, especially for figures, because it can name each entry as it's entered. Proofreaders, too, may find it useful: In direct proofreading, synthesized speech technology can provide an extra step—listening after looking—to catch errors the eye can miss, such as omissions or transpositions. In comparison proofreading, it requires the proofreader and the corrector to work in reverse. That is, the program reads aloud the *new* version—the one entered into the computer—while the proofreader marks the *old* version to show the *errors,* not the *corrections*. In the following example, the marks in the old version show the errors in the new version that the speech synthesizer has revealed to the proofreader as it read aloud.

Our squeegee, with a contoured wood handle that allows long use without muscle strain and a top-quality rubber blade that is not affected by oil, benzene, varnish, or lacquer, is the best on the market.

Old Version

Marked by Proofreader to Show Errors
in New Version

Our squeegee, with a contoured wood handle that allows long sue without muscle stain and a pot-quality rubber blade than is not affected by oil, benzene, vanish, or lacquer, is the best on the best on the market.

New Version

Read Aloud from Electronic Input
by Speech Synthesizer

How to Take Care of a Manuscript

These are the ways to keep a manuscript clean and easy to follow:

- Use a soft, erasable pencil of a deep color that photocopies well.

- Keep the original copy readable. Don't obliterate words with heavy marks; don't cover them with paste-ups.

- Write additions and replacements clearly. Distinguish capital from lowercase letters; show words as units; put space between words. Write only what you want to see: Don't write abbreviations or symbols if you want to see the whole word.

- Ring messages and instructions. Write them clearly. Use only abbreviations you know will be understood.

- Correct your own written errors unmistakably. Stet them, erase or opaque them completely, or cover them with adhesive correcting tape.

- Where there is enough space between lines, use text marks. Write additions and replacements above the lines, not below.

- Where there is not enough space between lines, use margin marks.

- Avoid writing vertically on the page or writing on the back of a page.

- Type a separate full-size sheet with material that is too long to write in the space between lines. Show clearly where it belongs.

- Keep pages the same size.

- Retype copy that your marks and erasures have made too messy to follow easily. Proofread your typing carefully.

- Be sure pages stay numbered in sequence. Mark added pages with an ABC code (*24A, 24B*), and refer on previous pages to the added page numbers (*24, 24A next*).

- Account for missing pages. For example, if you withhold a page to get it approved or to get current data, replace it with a sheet explaining where the right page is.

- Don't discard pages that have been crossed out for deletion, and do keep running page numbers.

- Protect the manuscript. Don't put it on a surface with anything that could spill. Keep it and deliver it in a container— a folder, envelope, or box.

12. What's Expected of You

Chapter

12

What's Expected of You

In Chapter 2 you were advised to proofread everything at least three times:

- First, proofread to catch errors in spelling, grammar, and usage.

- Second, proofread to catch departures from good typographic practice, such as bad breaks at the ends of lines or pages, misalignment, or inconsistent spacing between characters, words, or lines.

- Third, proofread to be sure everything makes sense—the words in their context and in their presentation in type.

Proofread to Catch Errors in Spelling

Today's spelling, according to *Merriam-Webster's Dictionary of English Usage,* "is a mishmash of archaism, reform, error, and accident, and it is unsurprising that not everyone who is heir to the tradition can handle it perfectly. Even so, with all the aids available to the poor speller, including electronic spell checkers, you might think there would be very few misspellings found in print. But the opposite is true."

You need to be reasonably good at spelling. At the very least, you should be aware of the words you can't spell and look them up every time you come across them. And you should be aware that the spelling mishmash includes certain words that can be spelled correctly more than one way—those listed in dictionaries as equal variants *(judgment, judgement; plow, plough; cancelation, cancellation).* Accept a variant as long as it's the only spelling of the word in a single document.

Depend on a standard dictionary. But be aware that some no longer *prescribe* what's right and wrong—they only *describe* what is. For example, some spellings that once were considered wrong have appeared so often that they've made their way into descriptive dictionaries *(alright,* evolved from *all right; miniscule,* evolved from *minuscule).*

A computer spell check program will catch the old "spelling demons," a few of which are listed below. It's a good idea to be able to spell all the demons whether you use spell checking or not:

accommodate (2 *c*'s, 2 *m*'s)	liaison
balloon	manageable
beginning	necessary
cemetery (three *e*'s)	occurrence, occurred, occurring
changeable	parallel
commitment, committed	permissible
consensus	prairie
coolly (*ly* follows the whole word)	precede, preceding
	privilege
deductible	proceed, proceeding
defendant	publicly
dependent	recommend
drunkenness (*ness* follows the whole word)	resistance
embarrass	seize
exaggerate	separate
harass	sizable
hypocrisy	supersede
inadvertent	totally (*ly* follows the whole word)
indispensable	vacuum
irresistible	weird

The new spelling demons are the errors that spell checking doesn't catch—typos that make words *(Ever man fore him self)*, easily confused words *(affect, effect; loose, lose; consul, counsel, council)*, and homophones—words that sound alike but are spelled differently *(compliment, complement; peace, piece; there, their, they're; forward, foreword)*.

Any word with a twin or a near-twin should ring a warning bell when you come across it. But phrases can sound alike, too, and not only to partner proofreaders. Here are some examples: *why choose, white shoes; research in typography, resurgent typography; next door, next store.*

You may listen to the manuscript (with ear or mind), but you must proofread with your eye, not your ear.

Be aware that words that are transliterated from a writing system other than the roman alphabet—Arabic, Chinese, Russian, Greek, or Hebrew, for example—may have several acceptable spellings. (*Chanukah, Chanuka, Hanukkah, Hanukah,* and *Hanukka* are all in common use for the Jewish holiday.) Keep only one spelling in one document.

Proofread to Catch Errors in Grammar and Usage

Traditionally, in the publications field, editors have corrected the defects in an author's work, and proofreaders have corrected the defects in a typist's or typesetter's work. Because of the recent changes in editorial roles brought on by the computer, proofreaders may be asked to look for more than just typographical errors.

If you have the authority to mark or query errors in grammar and usage, keep in mind that it's often wise not to be too zealous.

You probably should curb the desire to change punctuation much beyond correcting such blatant errors as a missing period at the end of a sentence or a misused apostrophe (as in "Work is it's own reward"), or querying to ask where the missing half of a pair of parentheses or quotes belongs. And you should probably avoid tampering with commas, because their use is highly individual.[1]

Finding fault with grammar and usage is not always in your province. Spelling and word division, however, are.

Proofread to Catch Departures from Good Typographic Practice

Proofreaders have almost always had the authority to mark deviations from typographic specifications and appropriate standards. That part of the job description hasn't changed.

Catch Errors in Word Division and Faults in Line Breaks

Different word-division guides and different dictionaries disagree on what makes a syllable—the spot where a word break can be made at the end of a line (*mea-sure* and *meas-ure, stand-ard* and *stan-dard,*

---

[1] *Editorial proofreading,* a stricter form of the craft, involves some of the work formerly reserved for copy editors. If you are expected to correct or query moderate as well as blatant errors, see Chapter 13, Editorial Proofreading.

wo-man and *wom-an).* For consistent syllabication, stick to one reference work.[2]

Here are some rules for word division:

- Never divide on a single letter. Leave at least two letters before or after a break. (Higher standards call for three letters after a break.) Don't divide four-letter words at all. Here's how to mark words or syllables that should not break:

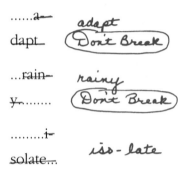

- Never divide a one-syllable word. Divide other words between syllables according to the pronunciation, not the structure, of a word: *ecol-o-gy, pho-tog-ra-phy, knowl-edge.*

- Don't allow the ending *ed* to stand alone when it's not a syllable. Here is how to mark such errors:

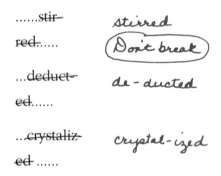

- Ordinarily, divide between double consonants—but not if it will break a one-syllable base word: *rob-ber, clas-sic, pos-sess,* but *crass-est, dwell-er.*

- Divide words ending in *ing* after the base word except when the base word is not whole: *call-ing, win-ning, han-dling, whis-tling.*

- Divide words that are spelled alike but pronounced differently according to their pronunciation:

---

[2] A good reference is the small booklet, *Word Division: Supplement to Government Printing Office Style Manual,* which provides 41 rules and an A-to-Z listing of hyphenated words. This guide, however, does not agree with any dictionary.

- attri-bute—noun (n.), as in

    His most admirable attribute is honesty.

- attrib-ute—verb (v.), as in

    They attribute their success to luck.

- Don't break these endings: *ceous, cious, geous, scious, tious, cion, gion, gious, sion, tion, sial, cial, tial.*

Here are some rules for line breaks:

- Don't allow a line break between a word or symbol and the figure or letters that combine with it:

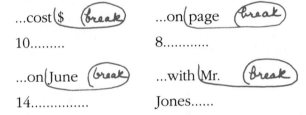

    ...cost $ (break)   ...on page (break)
    10.........   8............

    ...on June (break)   ...with Mr. (break)
    14..............   Jones......

But the following may be acceptable breaks:

    ...in Chap-   ...on Octo-   ...with Mr. A.B.
    ter 10...   ber 15...   Jones.........

- Don't allow a line break between numbers of fewer than six digits. Break larger numbers only after the comma or decimal, and use a hyphen:

    ...total of $434,982,-
    254......

- Ordinarily, don't allow a break in an abbreviation or symbol:

    ...on WM-   *WMAL* (Don't break)
    AL........

If, however, a break is unavoidable, certain symbols need no hyphen:

    ...section 7(B)(1)   ...$Mg(UO_2)_2(SiO_2)_2$
    (a)(i)....... $(OH)_2 \cdot 6H_2O$......

At times, the expense of resetting lines and the limitations of some computerized word-division programs offer a proofreader no choice but to accept an undesirable word division or line break.

Verify Typographic Specifications and Format

Be sure the copy you are reading meets specifications. You may prefer to check specs and do some other tasks in separate steps rather than as you read along. For example, you might begin by scanning each page quickly for obvious errors such as unequal line space or uneven paragraph indents, and then again to check running heads, and yet again to check word divisions and line breaks.

If you are proofreading by comparison, check the older version for attached memos, and check pages at their top, corners, and margins for notations and specifications.

Verify the following:[3]

- Does the copy follow the written specifications for type? (That is, if they're provided—and that's a big *if,* because you're more likely to have a finished document as a format sample than to have a spec sheet.) A spec sheet or a sample provides information on typeface and type size, width of margins, line spacing, and contour (flush, centered, justified).

- Are running heads (headers), titles, and captions correct and consistent in spelling, type style, and position?

- Is every head's format consistent within its level?

Note: Head levels may be specified in what's called a head schedule. Here's an example:

Level	
A	MAJOR HEAD
	all caps, ctr, empty line above & below
B	Major Subhead
	Clc, ctr, empty line above & below
C	<u>Minor Head</u>
	Clc, flush left, underline, empty line above only
D	<u>Minor subhead.</u> flush left, initial cap, underline, run-on, one empty line above the paragraph

If you're working on a long document and have no written specs, you may want to take notes on what you discover the format to be, including the head schedule, so you can more easily verify its correctness and uniformity.

---

[3] If you need to do typographic proofreading and are unfamiliar with the characteristics of type (for example, its size as measured in points, picas, and ems), see Chapter 14.

Verify the Appropriate Standards of Typographic Quality

■ Does spacing between letters, words, and lines appear equal?

■ Are paragraphs indented equally?

■ Do lines and columns align properly?

■ Does every justified line extend to its margins but not beyond?

■ Are there bad breaks?

- Widows at the top or bottom of pages or paragraphs?

- Heads that need to break more sensibly?

- Unacceptable word divisions or line breaks?

- Any line of text beginning with a hyphen,[4] a period, or anything belonging at the end of a sentence? A closing punctuation mark? An asterisk or other footnote reference mark? A superscript or subscript?

- Any line of running text beginning with a dash? (A dash may properly begin a line only if the line is a citation, a credit line, or a signature, or if it's used in place of opening quotation marks in a foreign language.)

- Hyphens at the ends of more than two or three consecutive lines?

■ Has the available equipment been used to its best advantage?

Proofread to Be Sure Everything Makes Sense

Besides keeping alert for material that seems to be illogical or to make little or no sense, a proofreader has these special tasks:

Verify Front Matter

If you are working on a document that has a table of contents or list of illustrations (front matter) or both, compare these listings with the text to be sure capitalization, wording, and page numbers match.

Verify Sequence

Look for errors in alphabetical or numerical listings, including page numbers and chapter numbers, as well as footnotes, illustrations, tables, etc.

---

[4] Such an error has been known to occur at a word break and even between the two hyphens that represent a dash in typewriter style.

Refer to a style manual (see the list in Appendix A) if you need guidance on which page numbers should be in roman numerals, what the standard sequence of sections is, and which sections begin on a right-hand page.

Verify References

See that references and descriptions match what's referred to and that none are missing, duplicated, or incorrect:

- Callouts. Be sure every table, photograph, chart, graph, map, or illustration is mentioned or announced (called out) before it appears and that it follows its callout as soon as possible. Be sure that every footnote[5] begins on the same page as its callout (reference) and that its number or symbol matches that of its callout.

- Jumps. Be sure that jumps, such as "Continued on page 2," are accurate.

- Captions. Be sure that captions and titles match what they describe—for example, that the number of names listed for a group photograph matches the number of people shown.

Check the Proofreading

It is often wise to follow proofreading with a checking step. Checking is better done by someone other than the proofreader. To check, a second person could do this:

- Review the marks to be sure they're understandable.

- Spot check line endings for word division and line-break errors.

- Reread the following places where typos are likely to be missed:
  - Conspicuous places—title pages, heads
  - Changes in type size or face—italics, footnotes, lines in all caps
  - Extra-long lines, extra-long words
  - Beginnings—of chapters, sections, paragraphs, pages. Read the first several lines.

- Take special care with the kind of text that seems to invite error:
  - Material in which errors would be costly to the customer, such as national advertisements or legal documents
  - Numbers, in words or figures, in tables or text, including prices, dollar figures, dates, percentages, simple arithmetic

[5] Footnotes appear at the bottoms of pages. Chapter notes appear at the ends of chapters. Endnotes appear at the end of an entire document.

- Text that discusses proofreading, typographic quality, spelling, grammar, errors, or perfection

- Anything in sequence—alphabetical order, numerical or alphabetical notation in lists, folios, footnotes, etc.

- Material that must follow its first mention in the text as soon as possible

- Material proofread or checked by the same person who worked on it in previous stages.

Check the Corrections

The probability of new errors being introduced in the process of correction or change is astonishingly high.

Be sure to check corrected copy against the previous copy's proofmarks to be sure all corrections have been properly made and no new errors have been introduced. Read a line or two before and after every correction. Check the top and bottom of each page as well.

Always check last-minute corrections, even the smallest.

Practice 19. Word Breaks

Instructions: Rewrite each word with a hyphen at *each place* it can properly be hyphenated at the end of a line. If no break is correct, write "Don't break." Compare your work with the answer key in Appendix C.

1. very_____

2. aviary _____

3. Wednesday_____

4. omit_____

5. bitmapped _____

6. planned _____

7. necessary _____

8. gladden _____

9. commit _____

10. controlling _____

11. referring _____

12. progress (n.) _____

13. progress (v.) _____

14. project (n.)_____

15. project (v.)_____

16. conscious _____

17. delicious_____

18. fictitious _____

19. avoid _____

20. emotion _____

21. thermometer _____

22. prism _____

23. distinguished_____

24. conquered _____

25. falling _____

26. collect_____

27. attempt_____

28. handing _____

29. crumbling _____

30. present (n. and adj.) _____

31. present (v.) _____

32. record (n. and adj.) _____

33. record (v.) _____

34. expansion _____

35. region_____

36. initial _____

Practice 20. Word Division Sticklers

Instructions: Rewrite each word with the hyphen changed so the first part of the division will not mislead the reader. Use only one hyphen. Keep prefixes and combining forms intact unless such a word division would break another rule. Compare your work with the answer key in Appendix C.

Examples: rein-vent *re-invent* pro-blem *prob-lem* re-commend *rec-ommend*

1. overop-timistic _____
2. knees-lapper _____
3. reap-ply _____
4. mate-rial _____
5. coop-erate _____
6. reap-pear _____
7. coax-ial _____
8. bio-graphy _____
9. bureau-cracy _____
10. de-privation _____
11. bet-ween _____
12. trans-cribe _____
13. in-frared _____
14. restruc-ture _____
15. no-thing _____
16. read-just _____
17. rein-force _____
18. ins-tance _____
19. ho-meowner _____
20. coin-cidental _____
21. re-storation _____
22. de-stination _____
23. anti-cipation _____
24. pro-fit _____

Part Four

Becoming Expert

13. Editorial Proofreading

Chapter 13

Editorial Proofreading

Grammar and Usage Problems

In both comparison and direct proofreading today, part of your job may be catching errors in English grammar and usage.

These are the areas to watch for:

- Grammatical disagreement
  - Between subject and verb

    Love and marriage ~~is~~ no longer every girl's dream.   *are*

  - Between pronoun and antecedent

    When everyone takes ~~their~~ seat we'll begin.   *his or her ? (or better . . . a seat /?)*

- Pronoun case problems

    ~~Her~~ and I worked together.   *She*

    The work was given to her and ~~I~~.   *me*

- Misused punctuation
  - Apostrophes

    Men's, women's, and children's favorite flavor is chocolate.   ✓✓✓

    The credit is all theirs'.   ✓

  - Hyphens and dashes[1]

    She's right/and she knows it.

[1] For an explanation of hyphens, short dashes, long dashes, and extra-long dashes, see Chapter 14.

> **Love is nearsighted.** When you are the writer, editor, or keyboard operator proofreading your own work, you will almost surely suffer from myopia. You are too close to see all the errors; get help.

Familiarity breeds content. When you see the same copy over and over through the different stages of production and revision, you may well miss new errors. Fresh eyes are needed.

Hyphens, short dashes, and long dashes can be con- *hyphen* fusing.

- Quotation marks

' single quote

He said, "When Gershwin wrote 'Rhapsody in Blue' ✓✓ he didn't think it would be popular."

■ Nonstandard usage and idiom

I'd change the world if I ~~was~~ king.   *were*

■ Faulty word choice

He is ~~literally~~ buried under mountains of paper.   *figuratively*

We expect our work to meet a single ~~criteria~~   *criterion* effectiveness.

■ Dangling participles, unclear antecedents, and other ambiguities

The witness saw the gunman shoot while parking.   *While parking, the witness (?)*

Matthew told Tim his phone was out of order.   *Tim, "Your phone is out of order." (?)*

■ Lack of parallel construction

The way to achieve good health is to exercise, eat right, keep busy, rest well, drink~~ing~~ eight   ✓ glasses of water every day, and maintain~~ing~~   ✓ a positive attitude.

A proofreader may need to do the research needed to be sure quotations are exact, ~~that~~ citations in a   ✓ bibliography are ~~done~~ accurately, and ~~on the correctness~~   ✓✓ ~~of~~ dates *are correct*.   ✓

Practice 21. Some Points of Grammar and Usage

When you have finished the exercise, compare your work with the answer key in Appendix C.

A. Disagreement Between the Subject of a Sentence and Its Verb

Instructions: In each sentence, underline the subject and the correct verb. Keep these rules in mind:

1. A singular subject takes a singular verb.

2. A plural subject takes a plural verb.

3. A collective noun is sometimes singular, sometimes plural.

1. Peace and plenty was/were promised by the new administration.

2. The title, as well as the subtitle, the author, and the publisher, belongs/belong on the first page.

3. The committee elects/elect its own officers.

4. The committee elects/elect their own officers.

5. At the office is/are a copying machine and a fax machine.

6. My boss is one of those unusual people who has/have great tact.

7. A part of the furniture for sale is/are antique chairs.

8. For this job, either of our typesetters is/are competent.

9. For this job, either typesetter is/are competent.

10. The office staff meets/meet every month.

B. Confusion Between Subjective and Objective Pronouns

Instructions: The subject of a sentence is in the nominative (or subjective) case; the object of a verb or preposition is in the objective (or accusative) case.

Underline the correct pronoun. Keep these rules in mind:

1. Use objective pronouns *me, him, her, us, them,* or *whom* when the pronoun is the object of a verb or when it comes after a preposition, as in *from me, to whom, for him, of them.*

2. Use subjective pronouns *I, he, she, we, they,* or *who* when the pronoun is the subject of the verb or when it appears after some form of the verb *to be* (or any other linking verb), as in *It's I, That was he, These are they.* (Example of an objective pronoun with the infinitive *to be:* Jean thought her to be me.)

1. There's a good new TV series for us/we police-story fans.

2. The table I reserved for you and I/me will be gone if we don't hurry.

3. Did you consult both he/him and she/her about your vacation?

4. Who/Whom are you writing a letter to?

5. She/Her and I/me met for two hours.

6. That was he/him on the answering machine.

Hyphenation Problems

A word may start as an open compound (two separate words), progress to a hyphenated compound, and end up as a solid compound (one word). Over many years, that's what happened to the word *proofreading*. It started as *proof reading,* an open compound; developed into *proof-reading,* a hyphenated compound; and ended as *proofreading,* a solid compound.

Dictionaries, unfortunately, don't always agree on which of the three stages a word has reached. The solution is to depend on one standard dictionary no more than ten years old.

Of course, no dictionary lists temporary compounds *(old-book collector, old book-collector),* and style guides disagree on many of the rules *(decision-making process, decisionmaking process).*

There is some light in this tunnel, however. Computers have given us a choice between *hard hyphens* and *soft hyphens.*

Hard hyphens are used in the spelling of a compound word, whether a permanent compound *(mother-in-law, twenty-five)* or a temporary one *(low-cost* housing, *many-splendored* thing).

Soft hyphens serve only to divide words at the ends of lines. And when the line width, type size, or typeface is changed, the hyphens should change, too. Here are examples of what can happen when copy is converted to a different line width:

- Original line width:

  When lines are reset and line width

  changes, line endings change and

  line-end hyphenation (word divi-

  sion) changes.

- New line width, hard and soft hyphens correctly set:

  When lines are reset and line

  width changes, line endings

  change and line-end hyphen-

  ation (word division) also

  changes.

- New line width, soft hyphens incorrectly retained:

  When lines are reset and line width changes,

  line endings change and line-end hyphen-ation

  (word division) also changes.

When you find superfluous hyphens, mark them for take-out as shown.

You need to know if the equipment or the operator whose work you see distinguishes between hard and soft hyphens. If not, to avoid future problems you may need to use a take-out sign to mark all the word-division hyphens at the ends of lines. Be sure to leave all the compounding hyphens in place, however.

Marks for Hard and Soft Hyphens

Type of Hyphen	Instruction	Mark	Example
Soft hyphen			
(divides a word at the end of a line)	Take out hyphen; make one word	Take-out sign	end-of-line hy-phen
Hard hyphen			
(joins elements of permanent or temporary compound)	Retain hyphen	(no mark)	end-of-line hyphen

Practice 22. Hard and Soft Hyphens

Instructions. Mark the soft hyphens for take-out; leave the hard hyphens unmarked. Compare your work with the answer key in Appendix C.

1. ......straw-
berry

2. ......anti-
biotic

3. ......anti-
inflation

4. ......bird's-
eye view

5. ......bell-
like

6. ......book-
keeping

7. ......gentle-
man

8. ......no-
where

9. ......your-
self

10. ......self-
control

11. ......two-
thirds

12. ......keep-
sake

13. ......anti-
American

14. ......cup-
board

15. ......cross-
stitch

16. ......sun-
shine

17. ......President-
elect

18. ......know-
how

19. ......nitty-
gritty

20. ......T-
square

21. ......sub-
sistence

22. ......main-
stay

23. The library hopes to re-
cover stolen books and to
put books with worn covers
back on the shelves after re-
covering them.

24. "The proofmarks are too
light to read. So please re-
mark the copy," John re-
marked.

Errors in Fact and Logic

You may be expected to check simple arithmetic (such as the addition of numbers in tables). You may need to do the research needed to be sure of the accuracy of quotations, citations in a bibliography, dates, or the spelling of people's names.

The *United States Government Printing Office Style Manual* reflects a standard policy: "If the proofreader detects inconsistent or erroneous statements, it is his or her duty to query them."

The policy doesn't make detection of "inconsistent or erroneous statements" a duty; the duty is to query when such statements are detected. A proofreader who's good at this kind of detection has a valuable skill.

These problems are among those to watch for:

- Misstated fact

  - Mistakes in simple arithmetic

    On sale: $6.00 each or 3 for $25   *$9 ea? 3 for $15.?*

  - Incorrect dates

    The United States entered World War II in ~~1914.~~   *1941*

  - Inaccurate quotations and titles

    Money is the root of all evil.   *The love of money (?)*

    Ode ~~to~~ a Grecian Urn   *on*

  - Mistakes in proper names

    Jane Austin   *e*

    ~~Ghandi~~   *Gandhi*

- Faulty logic

  My low opinion of myself reached a new ~~high.~~   *low*

  This field of research is so ~~virginal~~ that no human ~~eye~~ has ever set foot in it.   *new*   *being*

Finding problems of fact and logic takes the kind of mind that sees through children's jokes and riddles:

- How many of each animal did Moses take into the ark?

- What was the President's name in 1971?

- How much dirt is in a hole two feet wide, two feet long, and two feet deep?

    (It wasn't Moses, it was Noah. In 1971, the President's name was the same as it is today. There's no dirt in a hole.)

That kind of suspicious mind will catch the problems in such statements as these:

- Because of headaches, patients make about 18 million visits a year to a doctor.   *doctors (?)*
- SAT scores have dropped 500 percent.   *Ok? 100% would be zero)*
- He has turned 360 degrees around from his life of crime.   *180 (?)*

Consistency Problems

An editorial style (sometimes called a house style or a press style) is a set of choices for the mechanics of writing.

Style guides and style sheets codify the choices for abbreviation (p.m., P.M., PM, or small caps P.M. or PM), capitalization (the Committee, the committee), compounding (copy edit, copy-edit, copyedit), use of figures or words for numbers (ten people, 10 people), certain features of punctuation and spelling (Dickens's books, Dickens' books; catalog, catalogue), and some matters of vocabulary (memoranda, memorandums).

A carefully prepared document is consistent in editorial style. But a competent proofreader won't try to change the writer's choices (when they are clear) unless the publisher or office prescribes something different.

You have already seen an example of this book's editorial style—the use of the serial comma.

    Serial comma: spelling, grammar, and usage.

    No serial comma: spelling, grammar and usage.

You seldom see the serial comma (also called a series comma) in newspapers or magazines; the style guides that newspaper reporters and other journalists use call for it only when needed for clarity. Other style guides, however, specify the serial comma, especially those guides designed for academic or technical writing. If you have a choice, either style is correct; the important thing is to be consistent.

Organizations that prefer not to leave style decisions to individual writers may specify a style guide or put out one of their own. Several style manuals are listed in Appendix A.

Some elements of editorial style can be complicated. A little knowledge can be as bad as none; for example, the following sentences, each of which follows an accepted style guide, might be mistakenly marked for correction. Querying, as shown, is safer:

- Canadian schools teach both British and (U.S) spelling, but most Canadian writers prefer British forms to those of the United States.

  (Not inconsistent: "U.S." is an adjective; "United States" is a noun.)

- Some full-time personnel may prefer to work (part time) in the summer.

  (Not inconsistent: "full-time" is a unit modifier—a compound adjective immediately preceding a noun; "part-time" is a predicate adverb.)

To style a document, you need to know when to choose between equally correct usages, to keep track of the choices, and to make the same choice consistently. To do this well, you must know your way around at least one style guide. With or without a style guide, you may find it useful to keep a style sheet—usually just an alphabetical record of the choices you make in capitalization, hyphenation, abbreviation, and so on.

Practice 23. What's Wrong?

Instructions: Write out your suggested corrections to the problems, and add question marks to make them queries.

A. Checking Facts

Example:

You can't (?)

~~If you're going to~~ stay on this corner, you'll have to move on.

1. The triplets were named Anne, Barbara, Charlotte, and Dolores.

2. I want to travel outside the United States, even if it's just to Canada or New Mexico.

3. The profits shall be equally divided among the subsidiaries and the remainder shall go to the main office.

4. Mr. Speaker, I boldly answer in the affirmative—No!

5. Monday's lecture is canceled, but it will be repeated Tuesday.

6. In Chicago, two-thirds of the audience came from the city, and half from the suburbs.

7. Seven letters of the Roman alphabet are still used as numerals today: C, D, I, L, V, and X. For example, the pages of the front matter in books are usually numbered in lowercase Roman numerals (i, ii, iii, v). And paper dealers use C, D, and M to indicate the weight or unit cost of paper stock per 100, 500, or 1,000 sheets.

B. Checking Consistency

Example:

3 (?)   yd (?)

~~Three~~ ft. = 1 ~~yard~~

The Secretary of the Committee announced that the next committee meeting will be held at the treasurer's office on March 23rd. To get there, take 4th St. east to Main Street. Turn left into the Shopping Center. Park on the North side of the shopping center, enter the bank building, and go to the 2nd door on the right on the third floor.

> **_Figures can speak louder than words._** Misprints in figures (numerals) can be catastrophic. Take extraordinary care with dollar figures and dates and with figures in statistics, tables, or technical text. Read all numerals character by character; for example, read *1995* as *one nine nine five*. Be sure any figures in your handwriting are unmistakable.

Proofreading Tables

Some people can't remember a seven-digit phone number long enough to dial it. But a solo proofreader often has to be able to remember much larger numbers. To compare a table in a manuscript with the final proof, try grouping the numbers. For example, read *132435465* as *132 435 465*. Most people can learn to handle eight-digit numbers quickly; you should aim higher.

What to Check

Be sure to include the following among the checks you make when you proofread a table:

Alignment. Each column should line up in a way that suits its contents—centered, right aligned, left aligned, aligned on the decimal, or aligned on a common character such as a dash.

2–3	9	$ 1.25	I
22–33	10	19.00	II
222–333	100	300.79	III

Simple Arithmetic. Use a calculator to check addition or subtraction.

Consistent Style. Verify the uniform use of caps, punctuation (especially colons, terminal periods, and commas in four-figure numbers), abbreviations, and the treatment of blank cells (dashes, zeroes).

Footnote Reference and Sequence. Footnote reference numbers or symbols should follow from left to right and should match those in the footnotes.

Rules. Horizontal rules are used like underscores or to separate sections such as heads and footnotes. Vertical rules, used to separate columns, may appear in a draft but should usually be left out of final copy where spacing clearly separates columns. Straddle rules (crossing more than one column) may be needed for clarity:

Responses
<u>Yes</u> <u>No</u>

add rule to straddle 2 cols

Proofreading Artwork

Check artwork—photographs, drawings, graphs, maps, and any other kind of illustration—for the following:

- Position

- Size

- Accuracy of callout and description, in the text, title, and caption

- Consistency in type style with other artwork of the same kind.

Note: Be sure photos face the right direction; it's not uncommon for them to be mistakenly flipped.

Two plus two is twenty-two. The simplest math can go wrong. Do not trust percentages or fractions or the "total" lines in tables. Watch for misplaced decimal points. Use your calculator.

Practice 24. Table

Instructions: Compare the handwritten copy with the typeset copy. Mark the typeset copy for correction. Compare your work with the answer key in Appendix C.

	1	2	3	4	5	6
1			Toonerville Sales Company			
2			Balance Sheet			
3			December 31, 1994			
4			Assets			
5						
6	Current Assets:					
7	Cash				$9,700	
8	Accounts Receivable				4,300	
9	Merchandise Inventory				16,560	
10	Prepaid Insurance				1,200	
11	Prepaid Rent				7,500	$39,260
12	Total Current Assets					
13	Plant and Equipment:					
14	Store Equipment		$10,000		$9,000	
15	Less Accumulated Depreciation		1,000			
16	Office Equipment		$9,750			
17	Less Accumulated Depreciation		1,950		7,800	
18	Truck		$10,000			
19	Less Accumulated Depreciation		410		9,590	
20	Total Plant and Equipment					$26,390
21	Total Assets					$65,650
22	Liabilities					
23	Current Liabilities:					
24	Accounts Payable				$4,100	
25	Salaries Payable				1,200	
26	Taxes Payable				350	
27	Total Liabilities					$5,650
28	Stockholders' Equity					
29	Common Stock, $10 Par Value 1,000 Shares Outstanding				$10,000	
30	Retained Earnings				50,000	
31	Total Stockholders' Equity					60,000
32	Total Liabilities and Stockholders' Equity					$65,650

Toonerville Sales Company
Balance Sheet
Decemeber 31, 1994

ASSETS

Current Assets:		
Cash	$9,700	
Accounts Receivable	4,300	
Merchandise Inventory	16,560	
Prepaid Insurance	1,200	
Prepaid Rent	7,500	
Total current Assets		$39,260

Plant and Equipment:			
Store Equipment	$9,000		
Less Accumulated Depreciation	1,000	$9,000	
Office Equipment	$9,750		
Less Accumulated Depreciation	1,950	7,800	
Truck	$10,000		
Less Accumulate Depreciation	410	9,590	
Total Plant and Equipment			26,300
Total Assets			$65,650

LIABILITIES

Current Liabilities:		
Accounts Payable	$4,100	
Salaries Payable	1,200	
Taxes Payable	300	
Total Liabilities	$5,650	

STOCKHOLDER'S EQUITY

Common Stock, $1 Per Value		
1,000 Shares Outstanding	$10,000	
Retained Earnings	50,000	
Total Stockholders' Equity		60,000
Total Liabilities and Stockholders' Equity		$65,650

14. Typographic Proofreading

Chapter 14

Typographic Proofreading

Catching errors and faults in typography has always been part of a proofreader's job. But typography is a complex field. In fact, its intricacies have increased since the days when printers took six years to learn enough about producing a fine quality page of print to complete their apprenticeship. Even more than in those days, quality standards in this computer age are complicated by the variety of type-producing equipment and by its continual development.

If you must do more than check a typeset document for correct word division and typographic consistency, you need this chapter's information on typographic specifications and quality.

Typographic Specifications

Type is measured two ways:

- Points and picas

    12 points = 1 pica

    6 picas = 1 inch (.99648 inch in traditional typesetting)

- Ems and ens

    1 em = the square of the type size in use (in 10-point type, 1 em is 10 points wide and 10 points deep)

    1 en = half an em (in 10-point type, 1 en is 5 points wide and 10 points deep)

The main formula for type specs includes instructions for the following:

- Typeface
- Type size
- Line spacing.

Typeface Characteristics	
Size	12-point Times
	14-point Times
	18-point Times
Width	14-point Times condensed
	14-point Times expanded
Weight	Times regular
	Times bold
Decorative effect	Times outline
	Times shadow

Here is an example:

Times New Roman 10/12 × 30

This reads as "Times New Roman ten on twelve times thirty" and specifies the name of the typeface, the type size in points, the line spacing in points, and the line measure in picas, respectively.

In the given example, "10/12," the specification for type size and line spacing (also called *leading,* pronounced "ledding"), is an instruction to set 10-point type on a 12-point line—that is, to set 2 points of line space between lines of 10-point type.

The specification for the *line measure* or *line length* or *column width,* "× 30," is an instruction to set type in a line measuring 30 picas across.

Sometimes specs include both *primary leading,* the leading between lines, and *secondary leading,* the leading around heads, which is shown in parentheses in this example:

Times New Roman 10/12 (14) × 30

Typeface Characteristics

There are thousands of typefaces; and more are being designed constantly by professional and amateur designers. This chapter offers only a hasty glimpse into a very few of the varieties of type you may be called upon to proofread.

Roman type comes in two main varieties—serif and sans serif. Serifs are the small finishing strokes at the tops and bottoms of characters. A sans serif *(sans* is the French word for *without)* has block letters. Here are two typical Roman typefaces in their 18-point size:

Times New Roman is a serif typeface.
Helvetica is a sans serif typeface.

Many typefaces come in families or fonts, each of which is a complete collection of all the related alphabets in one typeface, including punctuation and accents. In a typeface used for running text, a family can include roman (which is the style implied if nothing else is specified), italic, and different weights and widths (as explained below).

Some common computer applications can modify characters in a single electronic font to create variations in size, weight, and width; they can also provide decorative effects such as outlines or shadows.

Some sophisiticated programs can customize type with great diversity. They have the ability to convert one style of type into another, such as making a serif face into a sans serif face, or changing the optical size of characters.

Weight refers to how heavy the lines of a typeface are. Within a family of type, weights can be named lightface, regular or medium (which is implied if no other weight is specified), extra-light, semi-light, demi-bold, bold, extra-bold, and ultra-bold. Sometimes other terms are used—book, heavy, black, or even loud, coarse, or fat.

Width, proportion, or *form* refers to the horizontal size of a face. Within a family of type, widths can include normal (which is implied if nothing else is specified), ultra-condensed, extra-condensed, condensed, semi-condensed, semi-expanded, expanded (or broad), extra-expanded, and ultra-expanded. Sometimes other terms are used, such as narrow, tall, compressed, extended, or wide.

Type Marking

Type marks specify typeface, type size, line spacing, and type style. These are standard type marks for style:

bf—boldface	**ital**—italic
C+sc—caps and small caps	**lc**—lowercase
Clc—caps and lowercase	**rom**—roman
reg—regular	**sc**—small caps
caps—capital letters	**lf**—lightface

Page Proportions

The paper page's width and depth are usually specified in inches, the type page's in picas and points. In some DTP programs, the type page is specified in inches, centimeters, or pixels (short for "picture elements," the dots that create an image in digital type).

Contour

The contour of a page, passage, heading, or line of text may be specified as follows:

- Justified—flush left and right

- Flush right, ragged left, sometimes called right justified

- Centered

- Ragged right (implies flush left)
  Flush left (implies ragged right), sometimes called left justified.

- Less common contours include these:
  - Wrapped (text framing or fitted around three or four sides or just the top and bottom of a particular shape, such as a set-off quotation or an illustration)
  - Shaped (text set to form a particular silhouette—for example, a wine glass or triangle).

Ragged right may be set with a soft rag (with word-dividing hyphens to keep the right-hand margin reasonably even), a hard rag (with no line-end hyphens, resulting in a very uneven margin), or by thought unit (for example, in headings or sidebars).

Indention

For both ragged and justified type, indents may be specified as follows:

- Flush left or justified left—blocked, like the paragraphs in this book
- Paragraph—first line indented. In typesetting, the standard paragraph indent is one em; in typewriting, five spaces.
- Hanging—first line is not indented; all lines following it are.

Headings can be set flush left or centered with paragraph or hanging indents, or in many contours, including justified, ragged right, squared, staggered, in stair steps, or in shapes such as a pyramid, reverse pyramid, or lozenge.

White Space

Gutters (the space between columns and pages) and margins—top, bottom, and sides—may be specified in points, picas, or inches.

Quality Considerations

Image

The sharpness of the image and its color (blackness, density) depend on the medium and its effective use. Uneven density—words or passages paler or blacker than those around them—happens sometimes with cut-in corrections made from photographic proofs; when you find this problem, mark it *check density* .

Alignment

Check the following:

- Characters, lines, and passages—for horizontal and vertical alignment

- Adjacent columns and facing pages—for balance

  - Modular balance requires every line of type to align with that in the facing column or page or both.

  - Adjusted balance requires only top and bottom lines to balance.

  - Unequal balance (used in some informal documents such as newsletters) requires the top lines to align and bottom lines to be unbalanced by several lines.

- Backup—line-for-line alignment of the backs of pages with their fronts.

Spacing and Grouping

Check for the following:

- Bad breaks

  - Wrong word division

  - Ladders of hyphens

  - Widows, at ends of paragraphs and at bottoms and tops of pages

  - Lakes, rivers of white

  - Knotholes (blocks of same characters). Example:

    Text [marks are used on copy with] enough space for them [between lines; margin [marks are used on copy with] too little space to write [between lines.]

- Page makeup considerations

  - Uniform sinkage at chapter openings

  - Specified minimum number of lines on pages that end chapters

  - Specified minimum number of lines following a heading at the bottom of a page

  - Apparently equal white space around heads and other display text, especially on facing pages.

- Line spacing (leading) problems, such as conspicuously unequal space between lines on a page

---

Optical Size

The point size of a typeface is determined by the vertical space it takes. The optical size depends on its design. These typefaces are all 12 point, but their optical sizes differ.

Garamond   abcdef

Times   abcdef

Palatino   abcdef

Bookman   abcdef

Century Gothic   abcdef

Helvetica   abcdef

> To check for center-
> ing, fold the page in
> half, hold it up to a
> light, and see if the
> right and left edges
> align. Or measure
> each margin with the
> tip of a pencil and
> your thumbnail.

- ■ Word spacing signs of quality
  - – Equal space between words in any one line
  - – Easy saccades (eye movements from one word or line to the next)
- ■ Word spacing problems
  - – Unequal space between words in a line. (When quality matters, mark for equal space.)

    Unequal wordspacing is ∧ a ∧ particular prob-
    lem∧with   justified   typewriter-style∧type.

  - – Tight, narrow, crowded spaces between words:

    Tight wordspacing can make a line hard to read.

  - – Loose, wide, spreadout spaces between words:

    Loose   wordspacing   slows   the   reader   down.

- ■ Letterspacing (character spacing) signs of quality
  - – Kerning, or adjusting the space between characters so they fit together well. Different typefaces need to be kerned differently. Here are some common kerning pairs:

    Not kerned: Wa Yo To P.
    Kerned by 1 point: Wa Yo To P.

  - – Ligatures, or design units of two or more characters. These are the common ligatures and the ligatured diphthongs:

    Regular type: fi fl ff ffi ffl AE OE ae oe
    Ligatures and diphthongs: fi fl ff ffi ffl Æ Œ æ œ

  - – Hung punctuation. Example, with quotation marks in the margins:

    "Errors...intrude themselves in the
    most preposterous manner, when
    and where they are not wanted,
    turn sense into nonsense, and upset
    the wisdom of the lawmakers
    and the devotion of the saints."

    —*Inland Printer,* January 1887

- ■ Letterspacing problems
  - – Conspicuously loose space between letters:

    Text with loose letterspacing is hard to read.

  - – Conspicuously tight space between letters:

    Text with tight letterspacing is hard to read.

Hyphens and Dashes

Hyphen. Besides marking the end of a syllable when the rest of the word is to be carried over to the next line, the hyphen has these uses:

- To divide certain prefix and root combinations, especially when the combination is similar to another word:

  multi-ply (several plies), un-ionized (not ionized)

- To join the elements of some compounds, especially those containing a preposition:

  mother-in-law, will-of-the-wisp

- To join elements of a unit modifier (an adjectival unit before a noun):

  gray-green eyes, long-term loan, know-it-all expression

- To suspend part of a compound when used with another hyphenated compound:

  a 5- to 10-year plan, space- and ground-based weapons

- To link proper nouns:

  London-Paris flight

- To join the elements of compound numbers from 21 to 99 and to separate the numerator and denominator when spelling out fractions:

  twenty-one, ninety-nine

  one-third, *but* one thirty-sixth of an inch

Em Dash. The ordinary dash is an em dash (one em wide), also called the long dash. A double hyphen in typewriter-style copy represents the em dash. The dash has these uses:

- To mark an abrupt change or break in the flow of a sentence
- Sometimes to replace other punctuation (such as the comma) when emphasis is needed
- To introduce a summary statement that follows a series of words or a phrase
- Often, to precede the attribution of a quotation.

En Dash. When available, the en dash (one en wide), also called the short dash, replaces the hyphen for this purpose:

- To show range between figures, representing the phrase "up to and including," especially in page numbers, dates, and dollar amounts:

    pages 1–10, 1989–1991, $5–10, 8:00–10:00 AM

In some styles, the en dash has further uses, including these:

- To separate elements that are all figures, all letters (but not words), or combined figures and letters:

    Phone 703–558–7400, AFL–CIO merger, Figure B–2

- To link nouns when one element has more than one word:

    New York–London flight

- To link hyphenated compounds:

    low-calorie–low-cholesterol breakfast

Italics and Underlines

Underlines in typewriter copy and italics in typeset copy are mostly used for the following purposes:

- Display, as in headings and captions
- Emphasis:

    He will *not* authorize this sale.

- Words or letters used *per se* (as words):

    Mind your *p*'s and *q*'s; also all the other letters.

    Word is a funny word; *funny* is a funny word; any word is funny when you think about it.

- Titles of books, magazines, newspapers, plays, movies, works of art, and long musical compositions:

    I read the *New York Times* while listening to *Madame Butterfly*.

    Many a TV drama follows a *Macbeth*-like plot.

- Names of ships, aircraft, and spacecraft:

    We took a cruise on *The Love Boat,* and I got seasick.

- Foreign words and phrases that have not been anglicized (that is, are not in an English dictionary):

    Stuffy? *Moi?*

- Case titles in legal citation, both full and shortened form (v., for versus, however, is not usually in italics):

    Smith v. *Smitherson*

- Latin scientific names of genera, species, subspecies, and varieties in botanical or zoological names:

    Strawberries are members of the genus *Fragaria* in the rose family.

Be sure not to italicize the roman type in the endings of possessives, plurals, and so on:

    I like the *Romeo and Juliet*ness of *West Side Story*'s plot.

    I enjoyed the *bon jour*ing and the *ciao*ing I heard in Europe, but I'm glad to get back to *hi*ing and *bye*ing.

Do italicize punctuation following a word in italics, except for closing parentheses or quotation marks. Italicize closing punctuation marks only if it's sensible to do the same to opening marks:

Italic parentheses:	She had a rage for writing—a disease with a Latin name *(furor scribendi).*
Roman parentheses:	She had a rage for writing (a disease with the Latin name of *furor scribendi*).

Part Five

Summary

15. Practical Proofreading—A Summary of the Marks

Chapter 15

Practical Proofreading—A Summary of the Marks

Marking corrections or changes calls for common sense, clear instructions, and knowledge of how copy is produced and corrected. Follow these guidelines:

1. Mark the exact spot you want changed.

2. With a mark or a message ring, explain either what's wrong or what needs to be done.

General Rules

Text Marks

Use text marks only on copy with enough room between lines to write words legibly.

Mark errors twice:

- First, to show *where* to make a correction, mark right in the line of type (the text).

- Second, to show *what* is wrong or *what* to do at the point marked in the text, mark right above the error.[1]

Margin Marks

Use margin marks on copy where there is not enough room between lines to write words legibly.

---

[1] Exceptions: See the sections "Punctuation and Symbols" and "Transposition" later in this chapter.

Mark errors twice:

■ First, to show *where* to make a correction, mark right in the text.

■ Second, to show *what* is wrong or *what* to do at the point marked in the text, mark in the margin.[2]

- In general, what goes in the margin is what you would have marked above the error if there had been enough room.

- Mark in the margin nearer the error.

- Mark from left to right.

- Separate multiple marks with slashes.

List of Practical Proofreading Marks

∧	add here	#	space
℘	take out	¶	new paragraph
✗	replace character	⊂	close up, leave no extra space
x̶x̶x̶x̶	replace characters	⌢	close up part way
∿	transpose (exchange)	✓	note the mark in this line
◯	(message ring) follow instruction or explanation but don't type or set the characters inside the ring	(sp)	spell out the abbreviation, numeral, or symbol the word stands for

The Most Useful Technique—Replacement

Replacement fits many kinds of errors and problems and is often the clearest way to mark. Use it freely.

Mark a slash through a single wrong character in the text and write the correction above the error or in the margin nearer the error:

Text Mark	Margin Mark
Typ*o*s happen	*o* Typ/s happen

---

[2] Exceptions: Corrections that don't need space between the lines may be more clearly marked in the text, with a checkmark in the margin as a flag.

If a word has more than one error, strike through the entire word, and write the entire correct word either above the error or in the margin nearer the error:

Text Mark	Margin Mark
Typos ~~happily~~ *happen*	Typos ~~happily~~ *happen*

Strike through any group of wrong characters and write the correct ones above the error or in the margin nearer the error:

Text Mark	Margin Mark
Unhappily, typos ~~jsoorm~~ *happen*	Unhappily, typos ~~jsoorm~~ *happen*

Correct wrong word division by replacement:

Either Text Mark or Margin Mark
Unhappily, typos ~~ha-~~ ~~ppen~~, so catch 'em!   *hap-pen*

Spacing Changes

Adding Space

To add space between characters, mark a pointer in the text and a space sign above the error or in the margin nearer the error:

Text Mark	Margin Mark
Typos#happen	# Typos#happen

To add space between lines, mark a sideways pointer and a space sign in the margin:

Either Text Mark or Margin Mark
> Typos happen / Catch 'em if you can

Closing Up Space

To close up space entirely—that is, to take out all space—put close-up hooks in the text and, if you think it's needed, put a checkmark in the margin to call attention to the hooks:

Either Text Mark or Margin Mark

Typos hap‸pen   ✓

Use replacement where it seems a clearer way to mark:

Text Mark   **Margin Mark**

Typos ~~hap pen~~ *happen*   Typos ~~hap pen~~   *happen*

To close up space part way, that is—to take out excess space but leave space between words or columns—put the top half of a close-up hook in the text and, if you think it's needed, put a checkmark in the margin to call attention to the hook:

Either Text Mark or Margin Mark

Typos ⌒happen   ✓

Taking Out Type

In a line of text, mark the characters to be taken out with a slash or a strikethrough. Add a loop (the take-out sign) to the text mark or mark a loop in the margin nearer the error:

Text Mark   **Margin Mark**

Typos happen   Typos happen
Catch 'em if you ~~catch~~ can   Catch 'em if you ~~catch~~ can   ℓ

Use replacement for a short take-out if it seems clearer:

Text Mark   **Margin Mark**

Typos
~~Typose~~ happen   *Typos* ~~Typose~~ happen

Adding Type

Simple Addition

When you come across an omission in the text, mark a pointer at the spot, and write the characters to be inserted above the error or in the margin nearer the omission:

Text Mark	Margin Mark
Typos c*a*n happen	Typos cn happen *a*

Use replacement for a short addition where it seems clearer:

Text Mark	Margin Mark
Typos ~~cn~~ happen *can*	*can* Typos ~~cn~~ happen

Hooked Addition

Attach close-up hooks to an addition that belongs at the beginning or end of a word. Put a right-hand close-up hook on an addition to be attached to the beginning of a word. Put a left-hand close-up hook on an addition to be attached to the end of a word:

Text Mark	Margin Mark
Unhappily, *t*ypos happe*n*	Unhappily, ypos happe *t/n*

Use replacement if you can't quickly figure out how to mark for insertion:

Text Mark	Margin Mark
Unhappily, ~~ypos happe~~ *typos happen*	Unhappily, ~~ypos happe~~ *typos happen*

Long Addition

Don't write an addition longer than seven words on the page. First, mark a pointer where the addition goes. Then what you do depends on what kind of work you're doing and what will happen next.

If you're reading by comparison and you know that the corrector will see the original copy, write a reference in the margin:

(add from p. x)

If you're not sure the corrector will have the earlier copy to refer to, carefully type the long insertion or make a photocopy of it, attach it to the page or galley, and write a reference in the margin:

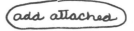

Punctuation and Symbols

Add punctuation marks in place with a pointer below and, if needed, a checkmark in the margin:

Text Mark	Margin Mark	
Unhappily,typos happen.	Unhappily,typos happen.	✓
Catch 'em if you can!	Catch 'em if you can!	✓

When a punctuation mark replaces another character, write it in place or draw it over the wrong mark if it will be clear. Mark a pointer under it and, if needed, a checkmark in the margin:

	Either Text Mark or Margin Mark	
Period written in place to replace exclamation point:	Unhappily, typos happen!	✓
Exclamation point drawn over period:	Catch 'em if you can!	✓

Transposition

Mark a double curve around adjacent characters or words to be transposed (exchanged), and if needed, make a checkmark in the margin:

Either Text Mark or Margin Mark	
Typos ahppen.	✓
Catch 'em you if can!	✓

Use replacement if transposed characters or words aren't adjacent, if more than one transposition occurs in a word or group of words, and wherever you think replacement makes the correction clearer:

Text Mark	Margin Mark	
Unhappily, ~~tpyso~~ happen *typos*	Unhappily, ~~tpyso~~ happen	*typos*
Catch 'em ~~can~~ you ~~if~~ *if can*	Catch 'em ~~can~~ you ~~if~~	*if/can*

The Message Ring—An All-Purpose Mark

The message ring allows you to do proofreading without special marks. First, mark an *indicator* in the text to show where the problem is.

Next, above the error or in the margin, write out and put a ring around the *explanation* of what you want done.

The indicator can be a pointer, an arrow, a bracket, a ring, or almost any mark that clearly shows exactly where the problem is. (Reserve the slash and the strikethrough for deletion and replacement, and use underscores only to mark for italics.)

The ringed explanation should say exactly what should be done.

Here are some examples:

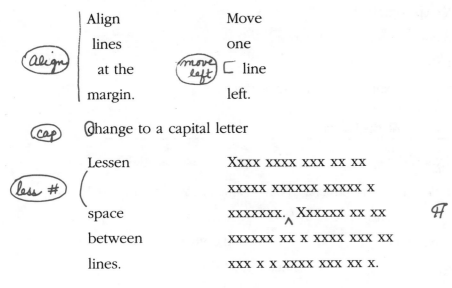

Abbreviations and Useful Messages

Some legitimate message marks are easy to learn because they are abbreviations. Here are common abbreviations used in the margin:[3]

(sp)   spell out abbreviation, numeral, or symbol

(cap)   capital letter (uppercase)

(lc)   lowercase letter

(c/lc)   caps and lowercase

(sc)   small caps

(c & sc)   caps and small caps

---

[3] Less common abbreviations used with professional proofmarks appear in Appendix B.

boldface

 italics

 center

Here are some instructions that frequently appear in message rings:

Move left	Move right
Move up	Move down
Align	Straighten
Move to p. x	Move fr p. x
Break (start a new line)	No break
ℋ (paragraph)	No ℋ
Stet (let it stand as it was before it was marked)	

Here are some examples of message rings:

	Marked Copy	Corrected Copy
(ctr hed/BF)	(Necessities)	**Necessities**
	When I get a little money, I buy	When I get a little money, I buy
(lc)	(B)ooks; if any is left, I buy food	books; if any is left, I buy food
	and clothes.	and clothes.　　*—Erasmus*
(Same line/ital)	—Erasmus	

Margin Marks with Kite Strings

Some forms of copy, such as tables with many columns or text with narrow line spacing and wide line length, are more clearly marked by using "kite strings." These guide lines, connecting the marks in the text with those in the margin, may help the person making corrections more readily find the spot where the correction needs to be done.

Some forms of copy, such as tables with many columns or text with narrow line spacing and wide line length, are more clearly marked by using "kite strings." These guide lines, connecting the marks in the text with those in the margin, may help the person marking corrections more readily find the spot where the correction needs to be done.

Appendix A. Recommended Tools and Resources

Recommended Tools and Resources

Tools

Pencils and Pens

Use a sharp pencil that marks in an erasable bright color.[1] Unless you are using only margin marks, avoid black, because it does not contrast with the type enough to call attention to itself. Choose a color that will reproduce, so the pages with your proofreader's marks can be photocopied.

For camera-ready copy, typed or typeset, use a pencil (or pen) of non-photo blue.[2] With normal pressure, a soft pencil will write a good, visible blue without leaving a furrow that will photograph, but its lead may be thick and blunt quickly. A harder pencil stays sharp and makes a neat, fine line; however, if you use it with too light a touch, its marks are hard to see.

You may want to use different colors—for example, red for corrections and bright blue for queries. Except for camera-ready copy, avoid a hard-to-read pale color like non-photo blue or light green.

Other Office Supplies

You may need the following supplies:

- Notepads for query and correction slips (self-stick notes like Post-its are handy and may be the best way to note corrections or queries on copy in its final stage, such as camera-ready copy)

- Paper clips, pencil sharpener, eraser

- Ruler or other straightedge to test alignment and to follow copy line by line (you may prefer heavy colored paper for this)

- Adhesive correction tape and opaquing fluid to cover marks made by mistake—when "stet" is inadequate

- Magnifying glass (for reading handwriting or small type)

- Typewriter, word processor, or computer (to create lists of corrections or queries or any insert or note longer than three or four lines)

- A good desk lamp, especially necessary in a windowless office (an incandescent bulb helps remove the glare from overhead fluorescent lighting).

---

[1] Good pencils are Col-Erase 1277 carmine red, 1291 indigo blue, and 1278 green.

[2] Good pencils are Eagle or Berol Verithin Non-photo Blue, 761½. A good pen is Commercial's nonreproducing light blue Illustrator.

Rules and Gauges

Because different typefaces of the same size vary in height and proportion, you cannot measure type size with a line gauge. You can, however, measure the depth of lines from baseline to baseline to determine the type size plus the leading (the space between lines).

Rules and gauges of metal or plastic are available at many office and graphic arts supply stores.[3] For typeset copy, you will probably want a precision line gauge that measures picas, points, and inches. Some come with marked intervals of 6 through 12 points; others have smaller intervals.

Reference Books

Desk Dictionaries

If your dictionary is more than ten years old, you need a new one. As of 1995, those listed here are the most recent editions.

These are the "big three" of the standard desk dictionaries:

Merriam-Webster's Collegiate Dictionary, Tenth Edition, Merriam-Webster, Inc., Springfield, MA, 1993. An updated abridgment of the *Third New International,* which has the largest database of any dictionary.

Webster's New World Dictionary, Simon & Schuster, New York, NY, current edition.

The American Heritage Dictionary of the English Language, Third Edition, Houghton Mifflin Company, Boston, MA, 1992.

Books on Usage, Style, Grammar, Punctuation, and Spelling

The New York Public Library Writer's Guide to Style and Usage, HarperCollins Publishers, New York, NY, 1994. Covers usage, confusable words, grammar, punctuation, style, indexing, typography, production, and printing.

Merriam-Webster's Dictionary of English Usage, Merriam-Webster, Inc., Springfield, MA, 1993. The most complete guide to questions of usage and confusable words available.

The Associated Press Stylebook and Libel Manual, The Associated Press, New York, NY, 1994. Standard journalistic style.

---

[3] Mail-order suppliers include Midwest Publishers Supply Company, 4640 North Olcott Avenue, Chicago, IL 60656, and APA Graphics Store, 1306 Washington Avenue, St. Louis, MO 63103. A calibrated magnifying tool, the Instant Type Size Finder, is manufactured by Service Engravers, 7 West 22nd Street, New York, NY 10010.

The Chicago Manual of Style, The University of Chicago Press, Chicago, IL, 1993. Emphasis is on scholarly publishing.

United States Government Printing Office Style Manual, Superintendent of Documents, U.S. Government Printing Office, Washington, DC 20402, 1984. Followed by many government agencies and contractors.

Word Division, Supplement to United States Government Printing Office Style Manual, Superintendent of Documents, U.S. Government Printing Office, Washington, DC 20402, 1987.

Books on Typography and Printing

Pocket Pal: A Graphic Arts Production Handbook, 15th edition, Michael H. Bruno, International Paper, Memphis, TN, 1992. The authoritative introduction to the graphic arts.

The Non-Designer's Design Book, by Robin Williams; Peachpit Press, Inc., Berkeley, CA, 1994. Covers the basics of typography as well as elements of good design.

General Reference Works

Consider putting together a small library of the kinds of reference books you need regularly. They might include any of the following: almanac, atlas, dictionary of biography, encyclopedia, foreign language dictionaries, street directory, telephone directory, *Who's Who,* ZIP Code directory.

Learning Resources

Self-Study Books

Harbrace College Handbook, Harcourt Brace Jovanovich, Inc., New York, NY, latest edition.

Spell It Right, Punctuate It Right, and *Errors in English and How to Correct Them,* three books by Harry Shaw (Harper & Row).

Mark My Words: Instruction and Practice in Proofreading, Second edition, 1993, by Peggy Smith (EEI).[4]

Substance & Style: Instruction and Practice in Copyediting, 1989, by Mary Stoughton (EEI).[4]

Formal Courses of Instruction

Correspondence, electronic, classroom, or on-site courses are available in many subjects, including English grammar, proofreading, editing, and publications design.

---

[4] EEI, 66 Canal Center Plaza, Suite 200, Alexandria, VA 22314-5507. Phone (800) 683-8380 or (703) 683-0683; fax (703) 683-4915.

Many cities offer inexpensive adult education courses, usually at local high schools. Many colleges and universities offer extension courses.

The Distance Education and Training Council will send a free pamphlet listing courses and schools in the United States. Write DETC, 1601 18th Street NW, Washington, DC 20009, or call (202) 234-5100.

Peterson's, an educational publishing company, can supply *The Independent Study Catalogue* by mail or lists of various courses in *The Electronic University*. Write Peterson's, P.O. Box 2123, Princeton, NJ 08543-2123, or call (609) 243-9111.

The *Official AWP Guide to Writing Programs,* which describes undergraduate and graduate writing programs, conferences, and centers throughout the United States and Canada, is published for the Associated Writing Programs at George Mason University by Dustbooks. Order from P.O. Box 100, Paradise, CA 95967, or call (800) 477-6110.

EEI, the publisher of this book, offers open registration courses at its offices as well as customized classes for clients in their offices nationwide. Classes cover all aspects of publication, including proofreading, editing, grammar, production, and desktop publishing; write or call for a current catalog. EEI, 66 Canal Center Plaza, Suite 200, Alexandria, VA 22314-5507. Phone (800) 683-5859 or (703) 683-7453; fax (703) 683-4915.

Appendix B. Professional Editing Marks and Proofmarks

Professional Editing Marks and Proofmarks

Because editing marks go right in the text, they are practical only where there is room for them; for example, between the lines of double-spaced copy.

Because proofmarks take little space between lines, they are practical in single-spaced or typeset copy. In the text they mark only the exact spot *where* a correction or change is needed; it is in the margin that they identify *what* correction or change is needed.

When you mark a manuscript (ms.) that will be rekeyed, keep in mind that some errors will not be reproduced and therefore need not be marked; for example, wrong font, defective characters, and some spacing errors such as unequal wordspace.

The following chart shows both kinds of marks side by side.

Instructions	Editing Marks (in text only)	Proofmarks (in text and margin)	
Operations			
Delete	to err is whuman	to err is whuman	
	to err is ~~not~~ human	to err is ~~not~~ human	
Delete & close up	to err is hummhan	to err is hummhan	
Insert	to err ^ human (is)	to err ^ human	is
		(for a long out)	out, see copy, p.x
Insert & close up	to er^ is ^uman (r, h)	to er^ is ^uman	r/h
Replace	to err it human (s)	to err it human	s
	to ~~hum~~ is human (err)	to ~~hum~~ is human	err
Transpose	to err human is	to err human is	tr
	to err is uhman	to err is uhman	tr
	(or)	(or)	
	to err is uhman (hu)	to err is uhman	h/u

Instructions	Editing Marks (in text only)	Proofmarks (in text and margin)
Special Marks		
Message ring: Don't set ringed explanation in type	(Same as proofmark)	Ring around message for example: $5
Let it stand (ignore marked correction)	To err is human *(stet)*	To err is human *(stet)*
Query to author	(Same as proofmark)	To roar is human *(err?)* (or) To roar is human *err?*
Counting slashes	(Not applicable)	Example: Mke sme correction consecutively as many times as slashes *a //*
Spell out	*(2nd Ave.)*	*(2nd Ave)* *sp*
Abbreviate or use symbol	*(Second Avenue)*	~~Second Avenue~~ *2nd Ave.*
End of document	*end* (or) *30* (or) *#*	(Same as editing mark)
Retain hyphen at end of line	...twenty- six letters	(Same as editing mark)
Delete line-end hyphen & close up word	...mis- takes do happen	...mis- takes do happen *3*
Space and Position		
Close up space	to err is hu man	to err is hu man *⌣*
Insert space	to erris human *#*	to erris human *#*
	(or) to erris human	
Lessen space	to err is human	to err is human *(less #)*
Equalize word spaces	(Same as proofmark)	to err is human *(eq #)*
Insert line space	(Same as proofmark)	Xxxxxxx xx xxxx xx Xxxx xxx xxxx *#*
Take out line space	(Same as proofmark)	Xxxxxxxx xx xxx xxxx xxxxx xxx *3#*

Instructions	Editing Marks (in text only)	Proofmarks (in text and margin)	
Move right	Ab|cd efgh ijkl	Ab|cd efgh ijkl	⌐
Move down	Abcd ⌊efgh⌋ ijkl	Abcd ⌊efgh⌋ ijkl	⌊⌋
Move left	⌐Abcd efgh ijkl	⌐Abcd efgh ijkl	⊏
Move up	Abcd ⌈efgh⌉ ijkl	Abcd ⌈efgh⌉ ijkl	⌐
Center	⌐Xxxx Xxxx⌐	⌐Xxxx Xxxx⌐	*ctr*
Straighten	Abcdefgh	Abcdefgh	*straighten*
Align	‖ Xxxx xxx xx xxxxx xxx xxx xxx xxxx xxx	‖ Xxxx xxx xx xxxxx xxx xxx xxx xxxx xxx	*align*

Line Breaks

Instructions	Editing Marks (in text only)	Proofmarks (in text and margin)	
Run on	(Same as proofmark)	Xxxxx xxxx ⌐ xxx xx xxxxx xxx xxx	*run on*
Break	Xxxx⌐xxxxxxxxx	Xxxx⌐xxxxxxxxx	*break*
Run over	(Same as proofmark)	Xxxxx xxxx x xx⌐xxx xxxxx xxx xxx	*run over*
Run back	(Same as proofmark)	Xxxxx xxxx *run back* xxxxx⌐xxxxx xxx xxx	
New paragraph	xxxx xxxxxx. ⁋Xxxx (or) xxxx xxxxxx. ⌐Xxxx	xxxx xxxxxx.⌃Xxxx	⁋
No new paragraph	xxxx xxxxxx xxx.⌐ *run on* ⌐Xxx xxx xxxxxxxx	xxxx xxxxxx xxx. ⌃Xxx xxx xxxxxx	*no ⁋*
Insert 1-em space	(Same as proofmark)	☐ Xxxxx xxx xxx xxx	
Insert 2-em space	(Same as proofmark)	☐☐ Xxxxx xxx xxx xxx	
Insert 3-em space	(Same as proofmark)	☐3 Xxxxx xxx xxx xxx	
Correct word division	⌃Perfection is inh- uman (or) Perfection is inhum-⌃ man	Perfection is inh- uman Perfection is inhum- an (or) Perfection is ~~inh- uman~~ *in-hu-man*	

Instructions	Editing Marks (in text only)	Proofmarks (in text and margin)	
Type Style			
Italic	Abcdef	Abcdef	(ital)
Small caps	abcdef	abcdef	(sc)
Full caps	abcdef	abcdef	(caps)
Boldface	Abcdef	Abcdef	(bf)
Caps & small caps	Abcdef	Abcdef	(c & sc)
Lowercase letter	Abc∕def	Abc∕def	(lc)
Lowercase word	ABCDEF	ABCDEF	(lc)
Capital letter	ABCdEF	ABCdEF	D
Caps and lowercase	abcdef	abcdef	(clc)
Caps and lowercase	ABCDEF	ABCDEF	(clc)
Wrong font	(Same as proofmark)	abcdefghijkl	(wf)
Subscript	H₂0	H₂0	$\wedge$2
Superscript	3³=27	3³=27	3$\vee$
Ligature	(Same as proofmark)	fly off	(liga)
Kern	(Same as proofmark)	Valued work	(kern)
Punctuation			
Apostrophe	abc's	abc's	⌄
Colon	Hamlet To be or not to be...	Hamlet To be or not to be...	:
Comma	To err, I say is human.	To err, I say is human.	⌃
Dashes, typeset			
en (short) dash	pages 10 20	pages 10 20	$\frac{1}{N}$
em (long) dash	To err well, it's only human.	To err well, it's only human.	$\frac{1}{M}$
3-em (extra-long) dash	Shakespeare, *Comedies* Tragedies	Shakespeare, *Comedies* Tragedies	$\frac{3}{M}$
Dashes, typewritten			
short dash (same as hyphen)	pages 10 20	pages 10 20	=/
long dash (2 hyphens)	To err well, it's only human.	To err well, it's only human.	--/

Instructions	Editing Marks (in text only)	Proofmarks (in text and margin)	
Dashes, typewritten *(continued)*			
extra-long dash	Shakespeare, *Comedies Tragedies*	Shakespeare, *Comedies Tragedies*	= ⑥ⓧ
Exclamation point	Wow.	Wow	set !
Hyphen	Nobody is error free.	Nobody is error free.	=/
Parenthesis, opening	To err is lamentably) human.	To err is lamentably) human.	⊂
Parenthesis, closing	To err is (lamentably human.	To err is (lamentably human.	⊃
Period	Proofreaders live by error	Proofreaders live by error	⊙
Question mark	Why.	Why	set ?
Quote marks, single*			
opening	'BATMAN' SIGHTED	BATMAN' SIGHTED	
closing	'BATMAN SIGHTED	'BATMAN SIGHTED	
Quote marks, double			
opening	Who said, "To err is human" ?	Who said, To err is human" ?	"
closing	Who said, "To err is human ?	Who said, "To err is human ?	"
Semicolon	Chicago, Ill. St. Louis, Mo.	Chicago, Ill. St. Louis, Mo.	;
Virgule (slash, shill)	$20/bushel *(slash)*	$20 bushel	/ *(slash)*

---

* As in a headline.

Appendix C. Answer Keys

Your marks need not always be identical to those in these keys. Many problems can be marked correctly more than one way. What matters is that you catch all the errors and mark them so what needs to be done is clear.

Key, Practice 1. Taking Out Type (Direct Proofreading)

A. Alphabet and Numbers

1 2 3 3 4 5 6 7 8 9 10 11 12 13 144 15 16 17 18 19 20

a b x c d e f g h i j k y l m n o p q r s t z u v w x y z

1970

19710

1972

1973

~~1837~~

1974

1975

1976

121977

B. Old Chinese Proverb

What your see, you forget.

What you heard, you rememember.

What you do, you do understand.

C. Brokern Patterns

Proofreading is little more than searching for broken pattterns. Of course, to be able to detect a broken pattern, ~~Of course, to be able to detect a broken pattern,~~ a good proofreader has to fully under-understand what the pattern is. That takes two kinds of aware-ness—of language and off type.

Note: You can correctly take out either instance of a repetition. Your marks may differ from the keys in this respect.

Key, Practice 2. Taking Out Type (Comparison Proofreading)

Comparison Proofreading Yesterday and Today

Before computers entered the process, a manuscript destined for publication was copied by typing on a keyboard, letter by letter, using a typewriter or typesetting equipment.

Proofreaders would then compare the newly typed or typeset version, letter by letter, with the manuscript.

In most cases today, computers have eliminated the age-old tradition of comparison proofreading. Word processed material is corrected error by error—without being entirely retyped. Typewritten or typeset material can be transferred electronically to a computer through a text scanner and then corrected error by error—without being entirely retyped. The electronic files can later be converted for use in desktop publishing or typesetting programs.

But errors can creep in during electronic conversion, often in the form of misread characters or dropped words or lines. And still today documents or parts of documents may be entirely retyped. It's still important to verify accuracy by comparing a final copy with an earlier version.

Key, Practice 3. Adding Type

A. Direct Proofreading

Alphabet and Numbers

a c d e f g h i j l m n o p q r s u v w x y z

1990

1991

1992

1993

1994

1995

196

1997

998

Sentences

1. If it's not chocolate, it's not desert.

2. The queen wore a tiara of diamonds and pears.

3. The speaker asked for the audience's divided attention.

4. We advise people with high cholesterol to eat more than two eggs a week.

5. Are we suppose to get use to thinking it's too much trouble to make mash potatoes the old-fashion way?

B. Comparison Proofreading

Printers' Measure

In traditional printers' measure, 6 picas = .99648 inch. In many desktop publishing systems, however, 6 picas = exactly 1 inch. The difference, .00352, or about 35 thousandths of an inch, is so small that you're almost always quite safe in considering 72 points equal to 1 inch.

Printers' Mesure

In tradition printers' measure, 6 picas = .99648 inch. In many desktop publishing system, however, 6 picas = exacly 1 inch. The difference, .00352, or about 35 thousands of an inch, is so that you're most always quit safe in considering 72 pints equal to 1 inch.

Key, Practice 4. Taking Out and Adding Type

Why You Should Prefer to Work on Paper

Paper is probably what you're used to. Most people can read words on paper much more accurately than on a computer screen—and therefore can do better at catching defects in printed words.

Paper is easy to handle. You can readily take it or send it nearly anywhere; you can quickly find your way through a stack of it; you can make inexpensive copies inexpensively so that each person in a group can look at and discuss the same document at the same time.

Paper allows simulation. You can mark on it to give the idea of proposed changes without actually making them.

Paper allows simulation. You can mark on it to give the idea of proposed changes without actually making them.

Paper permits commentary. You can readily distinguish between the text and the written responses to the text.

Paper provides a trail. You can see at a glance what the text was like before it was marked up. You can review your own work and approve or disprove it. And, keeping in mind that a writer wants—and deserves—to see what changes have been made, you can provide a record provide a record if you've worked on someone else's writing, or you can refer to the record if someone else has worked on your writing.

Note: Either is correct: make inexpensive copies inexpensively
or make inexpensive copies inexpensively

Key, Practice 5. Replacing Wrong Words and Characters with Right Ones

A. Alphabet and Numbers

a b *c*x d e f g h i j k *l*x m n o p q r s *t*x u v w x y z

~~won~~ *one* two three ~~fore~~ *four* fi *v*fe six

seven ~~ate~~ *eight* nine t *e*an eleven ~~swerve~~ *twelve*

1995

1996

1997

1*9*798

~~99~~*19*99

2000

B. Misspelled Words

1. cause and *e*affect

2. compl *i*ementary tickets

3. the capit *o*al dome

4. a half-~~carrot~~ *carat* diamond

5. gri *zz*sly bear

6. holier th *a*en thou

C. Spoonerisms

1. Young man, you have *m*hissed all your ~~mystery~~ *history* lessons and completely *w*tasted two whole ~~worms~~ *terms*.

2. It is ~~kisstomary~~ *customary* to ~~cuss~~ *kiss* the bride.

3. The poor man just received a ~~blushing crow~~ *crushing blow*.

4. He went to Portsmouth to see the *b*cattleships and *c*bruisers.

5. Have you ever nursed in your bosom a half-~~warmed~~ *formed* *w*fish?

202

Key, Practice 6. Marks for Special Replacement

A. Message Ring

1. Water freezes at 32° Fahrenheit. *[degree sign]*

2. The chemical formula for water is H~~to~~ O. *2 [subscript: H_2O]*

3. The chemical formula for water is H2O. *2 [subscript]*

4. Most keyboards show a dollar sign ($) but not a cents sign (¢). *¢ [cents]*

5. An English alphabet can be used to set the Spanish forms of address by adding a tilde (~) above the letter n (ñ): señor, señora, señorita. *ñ [n with tilde]*

6. "Fences" include opening and closing forms of these symbols:

   - parentheses: (and)
   - brackets: [and]
   - braces or curly brackets: { and }. *} [brace]*

B. Long and Short Forms

500 years ago, books printed with movable type sold for about one-fifth the price of ms books. The daybook of a Venetian book-seller in ~~fourteen eighty-four~~ *1+84* shows a stock of classics, religious works, schoolbooks, romances, & poetry. Dante's *Inferno* cost 1 ducat; Plutarch's *Lives,* ~~two~~ *2* ducats. Most customers paid cash, but Cicero's *Orations* was exchanged for wine, & other bks for oil or flour. The bookseller paid a binder with a copy of *The Life &
Miracles of the Madonna,* an illuminator with an arith textbook, & a proofreader with 3 books incl a Bible.

sp
sp
sp
sp 2×
sp
sp 2×
sp 2×

Note: As shown in item 5, mark for accent marks by writing the entire letter with its accent.

Key, Practice 7. Transposing

1. Mark "setup" to make "upset"

2. Mark "hangover" to make "overhang"

3. Mark "human being" to make "being human"

4. Mark "sky blue" to make "blue sky"

5. Mark "trail" to make "trial"

6. Mark "ingrain" to make "raining"

7. Mark "casual" to make "causal"

8. Mark "procede" to make "proceed"

9. Mark "calvary" to make "cavalry"

10. Mark "marital" to make "martial"

11. Mark "aide" to make "idea"

12. Mark "stake" to make "takes"

13. Mark "swing" to make "wings"

14. Mark "range" to make "anger"

15. Mark "grate" to make "great"

16. Mark "wired" to make "weird"

17. Mark "parse" to make "spare"

18. Mark "spare" to make "pares"

19. Mark "pares" to make "pears"

20. Mark "pears" to make "spear"

21. Mark "spear" to make "spare"

22. Mark "spare" to make "parse"

Key, Practice 8. Blatant Errors in Grammar and Usage

1. You should ~~of~~ *have* known that your name and address goes here.

2. I ~~disremember~~ *forget* whether your name or address go *es* here.

3. Your name, as well as your address and phone number, goes here now, ~~ir~~regardless of where the information used to ~~went~~ *go*.

4. Nothing would please her and ~~I~~ *me* more than to find at last a cheese-cake for ~~we~~ *us* dieters.

5. Just between you and ~~I~~ *me*, I don't read all the newspaper; I only read what I like.

6. I can~~'t~~ hardly believe that the fire burned for nine hours and required 500 firefighters to ~~be extinguished~~ *put it out*.

7. I heard the airplane *while* mowing the lawn, and I watched the accident, but I couldn't do ~~no~~ *any* thing to help.

8. Dear Mr. Soenso:

   This is a reminder about invoice number 9991 for $650.98 and invoice number 9991A for $1.29, which ~~is~~ *are* now more than 60 days ~~passed~~ *past* due. If ~~their~~ *there* are any problems with these invoices, please call me at once so we can correct ~~it~~ *them*.

   If your payment is in the mail, please ~~except~~ *accept* our thanks and disregard this letter. Thank *you* for your business and for you *r* prompt attention to this matter.

   Sincerely,

   Parker Plaice
   Account Represent *at* ive

Note: Item 2: Also correct: I *don't* ~~dis~~remember. Other solutions are possible also for other items.

Key, Practice 9. Review of Marks (Comparison Proofreading)

Proverbs

1. Rats leave a sinking ship.

2. Love me, love my dog.

3. Don't count your chickens before they're hatched.

4. Don't put the cart before the horse.

5. Don't throw a monkey wrench into the works.

6. Consider the ant, thou sluggard, and be wise.

7. Misery loves company.

8. Where there's a will, there's a way.

9. Fools rush in where angels fear to tread.

10. A cursed fiend wrought death, disease, and pain. A blessed friend brought breath and ease again.

Proverb ⌒s

1. Rats leave a stinking ship.

2. Love me⌐, love my dog.

3. Don't count on chickens 4⌐ before they're hatcheⱦed.

4. Don't put the cᵃt before the hoˢe.

5. Don't throw a monkey, ͢ *wrench* in⌐to the works.

6. Consider the sᶸᶸₘₐᵣᵈ, thou *ant* ᵃₙₜ, and be wiseⱦ.

7. Misery loves sᵞₘₚₐₜₕᵧ. *company*

8. Wᵉre there's a wₐll, theirs a ⌐way. *there's*

9. Fools rush in where angḙes fᶏre⌐to tradḙ

10. A cursed fiend wrought death, disease, and pain. A cursed fiend ᵞrought *blessed* ʳ ᵇ deathᵧ, disease⌐ and pain. *br* *ease again*

Note: Item 10: Your marks may differ from the key. Just be sure you caught all errors and marked clearly.

Key, Practice 10. Marks for Punctuation and Symbols

A. Missing Punctuation and Symbols

1. One inch equals 2.54 centimeters.

2. The program begins at 7:30 p.m.

3. For sale: table, $20; 4 chairs, $10 each; corner cupboard, $30.

4. Waste not, want not.

5. The door of success is marked with two words, "Push" and "Pull."

6. $2^2 = 4$, $4^2 = 16$, $16^2 = 256$.   *(superscript)*

7. We have not heard from you since we shipped your last order on February 28, 1995, to London, Ontario, in care of Mr. F. Galway. May we send our new price list?

B. Typewriter-Style Hyphens and Dashes

```
In bell-like tones, the ex-governor--the twenty-
first to hold office, announced the formation of
a semi-independent agency to aid the self-
employed.
```

C. Typeset-Style Hyphens and Dashes

In bell-like tones, the ex-governor—the twenty-first to hold office, *(dash)* announced the formation of a semi-independent agency to aid the self-employed.

Key, Practice 11. Review of Marks (Direct Proofreading)

Why New Proofreaders Suffer form Despondency

When you fist read proof you learn to your horror that you can miss, that perfection is an unreachable gaol.

Next, you learn that even when your work is perfect, not all the errors you caught will be corrected; that even when corrections are made, they aren't always done right; and that even when it was done right, new errors can occur. In fact, new errors can occur at any stage of production for many reasons beside human error, including faulty equipment (for example, interrupted electronic operation resulting for example in garble.

Last, the hardest lesson leaned is this: Others may be allowed to be imperfect, but proofreaders are not. Perfection, it seems, is a proof-readers duty.

The professionals in the publications business have known about this attitude for a long time.

Theodore Low De Vinne,[1] a distinguished typograper and type designer at the turn of the century, wrote, "The proofreader's position is not an enviable one....He may correct ninety-nine errors out of a hundred, but if he misses the hundredth he may be sharply reproved."

Benjamin Drew,[2] printer, scholar, teacher, and proofreader at the Cambridge University Press and than at the United States Goverment Printing Office, gives us this good advice: "Let no nervous or touchy man meddle with proofreading."

---

1. Quted from *The Practice of Typography, Correct Composition* by Theodore Low De Vinne, Oswald Publishig Company, N.Y., 1902.

2. Quoted from *Pens and Types* by Benjamin Drew, Lee and Shepard, Boston, 1889.

Key, Practice 12. Review of Marks (Comparison Proofreading)

Views on Error

Inland Printer (1887): Errors ... intrude themselves in the most preposterous manner, when and where they are not wanted, turn sense into nonsense, and upset the wisdom of the lawmakers and the devotion of the saints.

Dryden: Errors, like straws, upon the surface flow; He who would search for pearls must dive below.

Marilyn Vos Savant: While no one has yet figured out a way to eliminate human error, we always do the next best thing. We correct ourselves.

Sophocles: He who is not too stubborn to heal the ills his errors caused shows wisdom and earns blessings.

James Joyce: A man of genius makes no mistakes. His errors are volitional and are the portals of discovery.

Anon: The longer a man is wrong, the surer he is that he's right.

G.K. Chesterton: An error is more menacing than a crime, for an error begets crime.

Views of Error

Inland Printer (1887): Errors ... intrude themselves in the most preposterous manner when and where they are not wanted, turn sense ito non-sense, and upset the wisdom of the lawnmakers and demotion of the saints.

Dryden: Errors, like straws, upon the surface flow; He who would search for pearls must dive low.

Marilyn Vos Savant: While no one has yet figured out a way to eliminate human error, we do always the next best thing. We correct ourself.

Sophocles: He who is too stubborn to heel the ills caused by his errors shows wisdom and earns blessing.

James Joyce: A man of genius makes no mistakes at all. His errors are the portals of discovery.

G.K. Chesterton: An error is more menacing than a crime, for error begets crime.

Key, Practice 13. More Blatant Errors in Grammar and Usage

1. I smelled something burning, so I look [~~look~~ → looked] around and I seen [~~seen~~ → saw] smoke coming from the oven.

2. She don't [~~don't~~ → doesn't] know which of the files might could [~~could~~] be theirs [theirs].

3. I hunted for the information everywheres [everywhere] I could think of, but I don't know where its at [it is] [~~at~~].

4. I take my "breaks" in the smoking area like [~~like~~ → as] a cigarette smoker should.

5. When you take a message on the phone, you had [~~had~~] ought to ask this question: [;→:] "Whom [Who] may I say is calling?" [?]

6. The sales [sales'] force exceeded it's [its] goals and [~~and~~] which was commendable.

7. My teacher didn't [didn't] learn [~~learn~~ → teach] me nothing [~~nothing~~ → any] [^] about possessive apostrophes, so please tell me when I'm mistakened [mistaken].

8. Dear Mr. Soenso, [Soenso:]

This is the second reminder from us about invoice number 9991 for $650.98 and invoice number 9991A for $1.29, their [~~their~~] both of which comes [come] to $652.27 and which is [~~which is~~] are now more than 90 days [days'] overdo [overdue]. We are sending this letter by certified mail, return receipt requested, [requested,] to be sure you recieve [receive] it. Please get in touch with me right away so [^] we can straighten this out. We've got some sensational products coming up and we wouldnt [wouldn't] want you to loose [lose] out.
Hopeing [Hoping] for your promp [prompt] response.
Sincerely, [Sincerely,]
Parker Plaice
Account Represenative [Representative]

Key, Practice 14. Changing Type Style

Words About Words

A powerful agent is the right word.
——*Mark Twain*

Longer than deeds liveth the word.
——*Pindar*

Be not the slave of words.
——*Carlyle*

Words are stubborn. ——*Zartman*

Words make love.
——*André Breton*

A word, once sent abroad, flies
irrevocably.   ——*Horace*

People who say they love words
are the biggest bores of all.
——*Minor*

Words pay no debts.
——*Shakespeare*

Syllables govern the world.
——*John Selden*

Words purr, words roar; words
stir, words bore.   ——*Mateus*

Actions speak louder than words.
A picture is worth a thousand
words.   ——*Old Proverbs*

What masters of the language
know: Big words sputter; little
ones glow.   ——*Timothy Rufus*

Many a legal case or public question is settled by getting the words
right.   ——*J.S. Schultz*

Words (about) Words   (cap)

A powerful agent is the right word.
(——Mark Twain)   (ital)

Longer than deeds liveth the word.
(——PINDAR)   (clc)

Be not the slave of words. ——*Carlyle*

(*Words are stubborn.*)   ——Zartman   (Rom)

Words make love. (——**André Breton**)   (not BF) (ital)

A (Word, Once Sent Abroad,) flies   (lc)
irrevocably.   ——*Horace*

People who say they love words are
(the) biggest bores of all.   ——Min(o)r   (Rom) (ital)

Words pay no debts. ——Shake(S)peare   (lc)

(SYLLABLES) govern the world.   (lc)
——*John Selden*

Words purr, words roar; words stir,
words bore.   ——(m)ateus   (cap)

Actions speak louder than words.
A picture is worth a thousand words.
——Old (p)roverbs   (cap)

What masters of the language (*know:*)   (Rom)
(b)ig words sputter; (L)ittle ones glow.   (cap / lc)
——*Timothy Rufus*

Many a legal case or public question
is settled by getting the words right.
——*J.S. Schultz*

Key, Practice 15. Using Margin Marks (Comparison Proofreading)

Sentences A to Z

Each of the following sentences contains every letter of the alphabet.

- A quick brown fox jumps over the lazy dog.

- Pack my box with five dozen liquor jugs.

- Quick wafting zephrs vex bold Jim.

- The fox, jaw bleeding, moved quickly to daze his prey.

- Why did Max become eloquent over a zany gift like jodhpurs?

- Brown jars prevented the mixture from freezing too quickly.

- The bank recognizes the claim as valid and quite just, and we expect full payment.

- Judge Power quickly gave the sixty embezzlers stiff sentences.

- Zoe ma grand fille veut que je boive ce whisky dont je ne veux pas.

- Kaufen Sie jede Woche vier gute bequeme Pelze xy.

Sentences A to Z

Each of the following sentences contains every letter of the alphabet.

- A quick brown fox jumped over the lazy hog.   *s* *d*

- Pack my box with four dozen liquor jugs.   *five* *g*

- Quick wafting zephrs vex bald Jim.   *y* *o*

- The fox, jaw bleeding, moved quickly to daze his pray.   *e*

- Why did Max become eloquent over a zany gift like jodphurs?   ✓

- Brown jars prevented the mixture from freezing too quickly.   ✓

- The bank recognizes the clam as valid and quite just, and we expect full payment.   *i*

- Judge Power quickly gave the six embezzlers stiff sentences.   *ty*

- Zoe ma grand fille veut que je boive ce whisky dont je ne ne veux pas.   *g*

- Kaufen Sie jede Woche vier gute bequeme Pelze xy.   (cap)/r

Key, Practice 16. Still More Blatant Errors in Grammar and Usage

A. Danglers

1. Your invitation come [a] when I was busy moving my office and was mislaid.

2. He had a cough when he went to school along with a lot of other symptoms.

3. The new movie, "Dracula," terrifies everyone now showing at theaters.

4. The 36-inch telescope, will be use [cd] in a systematic search for supernovas designed by astrophysicists from Berkeley.

5. Hidden in the dining room breakfront in a box enameled with blue flowers, Mary Michael keeps the keys to 15 neighbor's houses.

B. Problems with Sentence Structure

1. I don't want nobody [anybody] working after five o'clock. [lc] The funds budgeted for overtime having [have] run out. (Also correct [and less stilted]: I don't want anybody working after five o'clock. The funds budgeted for overtime have run out.)

2. Don't waste motion; Work [lc] like [the way] I do [lc] With no extra effort, [lc] Just enough to do the job.

3. Dear Parker Plaice:

You have written me two letters saying that I owe you money. and you are mistaken. On September 1, the day I received the goods from you, I wrote check number 325 on the First Commercial Bank and Trust Co. for $652.27 and mailed it. you cashed it. it came back to me with my bank statement for October. it is in my files. Please check your records. if it will help resolve the problem, I will get a copy made of the check and send it to you.

Sincerely yours,

George T. Soenso

Key, Practice 17. Adding and Taking Out Space

A. One Word or Two

around	a round
be long	belong
ground cover	groundcover
a ward	award
vanguard	van guard
cardboard	cardboard
in exact position	inexact position

B. Sentences

1. The product often thousand times zero is zero.

2. We hope for better grow thin our low-calorie milkshake.

3. Proofreaders need many qualities; noon equality is most important. *no one quality*

4. We bough there very thing she wanted. *bought her everything*

5. She was incross mood because she had comecross crossword puzzle *come across a* she couldn't finish.

C. Paragraph

EVERY ONE who works with paper—and that includes those who's work involves gift rap, wallpaper, male, or any *whose* *w* *mail* kind of document—should follow this advise: Never shead *c* your work surface with aliquid that can spill. Experienced proofreaders can tell many an antidote about soggy proof *anecdote* sheets or dripping manuscripts caused by care less people ignoring that sample rule.

Key, Practice 18. Spacing Marks

A. The Republic of Letters

As ~~Washingt-on~~ Irving wrote, *Washing-ton*

"The ~~rep-ublic~~ of let- *re-public*
ters is the
most... ~~dis-cordant~~ of *dis-cordant*
all ~~republ-ics,~~ ~~anci-ent~~ *repub-lics*
an-cient
and modern."

B. My Lord the Book

A book is an aristocrat; 'Tis pampered—lives in state; (break)
Stands on a shelf, with naught whereat
(merge) To worry—
lovely fate!
Enjoys the best of company; And (break)
often—ay, 'tis so—
Like much in aristocracy,
Its title makes it go.

C. Invisible Writing

"Printing should be invisible," wrote Beatrice
type." Type, she said, should be a "transparent
Warde, that is, "Type well used is invisible as
goblet, a conveyor to look through, rather than
hide, the vintage of the human mind."

Writing, too, we say, should be invisible
and transparent, i.e., its meaning should be
(make all ¶ indents same) uncluttered and unclouded by grammatical, rhetorical, or logical misuse.

(move left) Words well used are the vintage of the
human mind.

Key, Practice 19. Word Breaks

1. very *Don't break*
2. aviary *avi-ary*
3. Wednesday *Wednes-day*
4. omit *Don't break*
5. bitmapped *bit-mapped*
6. planned *Don't break*
7. necessary *ne-ces-sary*
8. gladden *glad-den*
9. commit *com-mit*
10. controlling *con-trol-ling*
11. referring *re-fer-ring*
12. progress (n.) *prog-ress*
13. progress (v.) *pro-gress*
14. project (n.) *proj-ect*
15. project (v.) *pro-ject*
16. conscious *con-scious*
17. delicious *de-li-cious*
18. fictitious *fic-ti-tious*
19. avoid *Don't break*
20. emotion *emo-tion*
21. thermometer *ther-mom-e-ter*
22. prism *Don't break*
23. distinguished *dis-tin-guished*
24. conquered *con-quered*
25. falling *fall-ing*
26. collect *col-lect*
27. attempt *at-tempt*
28. handing *hand-ing*
29. crumbling *crum-bling*
30. present (n. and adj.) *pres-ent*
31. present (v.) *pre-sent*
32. record (n. and adj.) *rec-ord*
33. record (v.) *re-cord*
34. expansion *ex-pan-sion*
35. region *re-gion*
36. initial *ini-tial*

Key, Practice 20. Word Division Sticklers

1. overop-timistic *over-optimistic*
2. knees-lapper *knee-slapper*
3. reap-ply *re-apply*
4. mate-rial *ma-terial*
5. coop-erate *co-operate*
6. reap-pear *re-appear*
7. coax-ial *co-axial*
8. bio-graphy *bi-ography*
9. bureau-cracy *bureauc-racy*
10. de-privation *dep-rivation*
11. bet-ween *be-tween*
12. trans-cribe *tran-scribe*
13. in-frared *infra-red*
14. restruc-ture *re-structure*
15. no-thing *noth-ing*
16. read-just *re-adjust*
17. rein-force *re-inforce*
18. ins-tance *in-stance*
19. ho-meowner *home-owner*
20. coin-cidental *co-incidental*
21. re-storation *res-toration*
22. de-stination *des-tination*
23. anti-cipation *antic-ipation*
24. pro-fit *prof-it*

Key, Practice 21. Some Points of Grammar and Usage

A. Disagreement Between the Subject of a Sentence and Its Verb

Rules:

    1. A singular subject takes a singular verb.

    2. A plural subject takes a plural verb.

    3. A collective noun is sometimes singular, sometimes plural.

1. Peace and plenty was/<u>were</u> promised by the new administration. (Rule 2.)

2. The <u>title</u>, as well as the subtitle, the author, and the publisher, <u>belongs</u>/belong on the first page. (Rule 1. Don't be misled by words between the subject and the verb.)

3. The <u>committee</u> <u>elects</u>/elect its own officers. (Rule 3. It elects its own/They elect their own.)

4. The <u>committee</u> elects/<u>elect</u> their own officers.

5. At the office is/<u>are</u> <u>a copying machine and a fax machine.</u>

6. My boss is one of <u>those unusual people</u> who has/<u>have</u> great tact. (Rule 2. Of those unusual people who have great tact, my boss is one. Don't be misled by relative pronouns.)

7. A <u>part</u> of the furniture for sale <u>is</u>/are antique chairs. (Rule 1. "part" is singular.)

8. For this job, <u>either</u> of our typesetters <u>is</u>/are competent. (Rule 1. Literally, either one is competent.)

9. For this job, <u>either</u> typesetter <u>is</u>/are competent. (Rule 1. Literally, either *one* is competent.)

10. The <u>office</u> <u>staff</u> <u>meets</u>/<u>meet</u> every month. (Rule 3. Either way.)

B. Confusion Between Subjective and Objective Pronouns

Rules:

1. Use objective pronouns *me, him, her, us, them,* or *whom* when the pronoun is the object of a verb or when it comes after a preposition, as in *from me, to whom, for him, of them.*

2. Use subjective pronouns *I, he, she, we, they,* or *who* when the pronoun is the subject of the verb or when it appears after some form of the verb *to be* (or any other linking verb), as in *It's I, That was he, These are they.* (Example of an objective pronoun with the infinitive *to be:* Jean thought her to be me.)

1. There's a good new TV series for <u>us</u>/we police-story fans. (Rule 1.)

2. The table I reserved for you and I/<u>me</u> will be gone if we don't hurry. (Rule 1.)

3. Did you consult both he/<u>him</u> and she/<u>her</u> about your vacation? (Object of a verb, Rule 1.)

4. Who/<u>Whom</u> are you writing a letter to? (Rule 1. To whom are you writing?)

5. <u>She</u>/Her and <u>I</u>/me met for two hours. (Rule 2.)

6. That was <u>he</u>/him on the answering machine. (Rule 2. Linking verb)

Key, Practice 22. Hard and Soft Hyphens

1. ......straw-
   berry

2. ......anti-
   biotic

3. ......anti-
   inflation

4. ......bird's-
   eye view

5. ......bell-
   like

6. ......book-
   keeping

7. ......gentle-
   man

8. ......no-
   where

9. ......your-
   self

10. ......self-
    control

11. ......two-
    thirds

12. ......keep-
    sake

13. ......anti-
    American

14. ......cup-
    board

15. ......cross-
    stitch

16. ......sun-
    shine

17. ......President-
    elect

18. ......know-
    how

19. ......nitty-
    gritty

20. ......T-
    square

21. ......sub-
    sistence

22. ......main-
    stay

23. The library hopes to re-
    cover stolen books and to
    put books with worn covers
    back on the shelves after re-
    covering them.

24. "The proofmarks are too
    light to read. So please re-
    mark the copy," John re-
    marked.

Key, Practice 23. What's Wrong?

A. Checking Facts

quadruplets(?)

1. The ~~triplets~~ were named Anne, Barbara, Charlotte, and Dolores.

2. I want to travel outside the United States, even if it's just to Canada or ~~New Mexico.~~
   OK?

   Part of the (?)
3. ~~The~~ profits shall be equally divided among the subsidiaries and the remainder shall go to the main office.

   Yes(?)
4. Mr. Speaker, I boldly answer in the affirmative—~~No!~~

   given(?)
5. Monday's lecture is canceled, but it will be ~~repeated~~ Tuesday.

   another third(?)
6. In Chicago, two-thirds of the audience came from the city, and ~~half~~ from the suburbs.

7. Seven letters of the Roman alphabet are still used as numerals today: C,
   M (?)
   D, I, L, V, and X. For example, the pages of the front matter in books
   iv (?)
   are usually numbered in lowercase Roman numerals (i, ii, iii, v). And
   paper dealers use C, D, and M to indicate the weight or unit cost of
   paper stock per 100, 500, or 1,000 sheets.

B. Checking Consistency

Note: These are the inconsistencies you should have found and queried:

Capitals/lowercase:	Line 1—Secretary, Line 2—treasurer
	Line 1—Committee...committee
	Line 3—east, Line 4—North
	Lines 3–4—Shopping Center, Line 4—
	shopping center
Abbreviations/words:	Line 2—23rd, Line 3—4th, Line 5—2nd...third
	Line 3—St. ...Street

The Secretary of the Committee announced that the next committee meeting will be held at the treasurer's office on March 23rd. To get there, take 4th St. east to Main Street. Turn left into the Shopping Center. Park on the North side of the shopping center, enter the bank building, and go to the 2nd door on the right on the third floor.

Key, Practice 24. Table

Toonerville Sales Company
Balance Sheet
December 31, 1994

ASSETS

Current Assets:
Cash	$9,700	
Accounts Receivable	4,300	
[Merchandise Inventory	16,560	
Prepaid Insurance	1,200	
Prepaid Rent	7,500	
Total Current Assets		$39,260

(move left) *(cap)*

Plant and Equipment:
Store Equipment	$9,000 *(10)*	
Less Accumulated Depreciation	1,000	$9,000
Office Equipment	$9,750	
Less Accumulated Depreciation	1,950	7,800
Truck	$10,000	
Less Accumulated Depreciation	410	9,590
Total Plant and Equipment		$26,390
Total Assets		$65,650

(make indentions same under all headings) *(double underscore)*

LIABILITIES

Current Liabilities:
Accounts Payable	$4,100	
Salaries Payable	1,200	
Taxes Payable	305	
Total Liabilities	$5,650	

(move right)

STOCKHOLDERS' EQUITY

Common Stock, $10 Par Value		
1,000 Shares Outstanding	$10,000	
Retained Earnings	50,000	
Total Stockholders' Equity		60,000
Total Liabilities and Stockholders' Equity		$65,650

Index